Praise for Single Man, Married Man from Media & Readers:

"It's a fun read!!!" – **NBC The TODAY Show**

"Dating advice to women from eight different men. Are you rolling your eyes? We were too, until we read "Single Man Married Man" and met the group of authors all ranging from single to divorced. These are the men who are offering their solid advice on dating. And just in case you want to make a Steve Harvey comparison *cough* "Think Like A Man" *cough* don't! This book is allowing women to take a peek inside the minds of real men and how they perceive us." - **HelloBeautiful.com**

"Absolutely love this book! This book is knowledge on relationships & also self-reflection. I have nothing negative to say about this book. I hope there's a Single Woman, Married Woman in the works!"- **Tiffany (Maryland)**

"Many women may consider a must read" – **FOX News**

"This is my first time ever leaving a review for an online purchase, but I felt it was necessary to leave one for this book. The book is absolutely a must read and simply amazing! Usually I read books about foreign rela~~tions~~ ~~poli~~tics, and steer away from rel~~ationships~~ e reading the book, I had a good understanding of how men think. However the book essentially pointed something out that I didn't realize, at the end of the day, men and women all want the same thing." - **Sarah (Houston, TX)**

"As I said it is written by men but it is something that both sexes can relate to, because it shows the importance of honestly, communication and dedication to a common goal. Both the man and the woman have to be willing to let themselves be a little vulnerable, allowing the other person in. They both need to really listen and not judge the current situation by their past dating experiences." - **Cyrus (Mississippi)**

"You gentlemen are definitely going to heal a lot of broken homes and relationships. When I finally started reading my copy that I purchased at the Love Lust Relationships panel event I was blown away from the first few pages. As I got deeper into the book I became more and more in touch with it and felt connected to almost everything on the pages that I experience with my wife." - **Shawn (Brooklyn, New York)**

Because of this book, I look forward to dating and the steps it takes to have a successful and lasting relationship! I am finally able to feel confident about my dating life---here's to finding real love."
Barbara aka Roxie, radio personality Radio 103.9 NY

SINGLE MAN, MARRIED MAN

EVERY MAN WANTS TO GET MARRIED - WHY NOT TO YOU?

By

Jean Alerte, Jickael Bazin, Frank Gateau, Rae Holliday, Zangba Thomson, Fadelf Jackson, Kel Spencer, and Pervis Taylor III

Citadelle Publishing LLc
441 Marcus Garvey Blvd, Brooklyn, NY 11216
www.Citadellebooks.com

Please visit www.singlemanmarriedman.com for information regarding tour dates, bookings, and speaking engagements for Dr. Jean Alerte, Jickael Bazin, Frank Gateau and Rae Holliday.

Cover designed by Bang
Photography by Jonathan "Outerfocus" Ortiz
Cover Model Appearances: (Front Cover) Dr. Jean Alerte, Gayna Alerte, Barbara "Roxie" De Laleu, Inia Estima, Karen Tappin-Saunderson and Damani Saunderson (Back Cover) Jickael Bazin, David Hong Esq, Rae Holliday, Frank Gateau, Kemar Cohen.

Zangba Thomson appears courtesy of Bong Mines Entertainment LLC & Zangba Thomson Productions.

Copy Editor: Zangba Thomson

ISBN: 1502955318
ISBN 13: 9781502955319
Library of Congress Control Number: 2014919113
CreateSpace Independent Publishing Platform
North Charleston, South Carolina

CONTENTS

Joe,
Live Laugh + Love w/ Passion   5/29/15

SINGLE MAN, MARRIED MAN

EVERY MAN WANTS TO GET MARRIED - WHY NOT TO YOU?

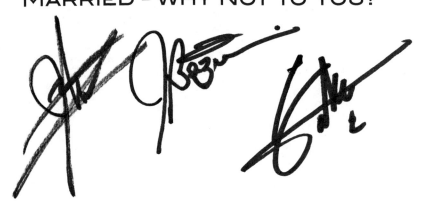

FOREWORD

The wonderful thing about human behavior is—people change—and that's an absolute blessing. I can remember the wonderful moment when I proposed to my wife and she said, "Yes!" And many years later, I'm extremely grateful to see the beauty in our ups and downs, and in our strengths and weaknesses. This in-depth observance of our trials and triumphs has helped us to manage our expectations of each other; and as responsible parents—it has also aided us in being aware of the sudden changes, growth and well being of our child. A relationship is a team effort, and I want my wife to win also. If she wins—I win, and that's why I'm grateful to Dr. Jean Alerte and the other co-authors for writing *Single Man, Married Man* because this book gives the reader an opportunity to see the underlying current and future needs that exist in a single male—in search of finding a great wife. *Single Man, Married Man* makes it clear that if you want to be heard—you have to observe and listen, not only to words but also to your partner's behavior. Great work gentlemen!

JAMIE HECTOR
ACTOR | PRODUCER | PHILANTHROPIST

PREFACE

The *Single Man, Married Man* (SMMM) movement began with Frank Gateau and Dr. Jean Alerte in Brooklyn, New York, when a lady friend of theirs asked, "How is it that the two of you grew up together, are best friends, and work so closely with each other, but Jean is married; he's all about his wife, being in love, and bringing people together; but Frank, on the other hand, seems like the total opposite—someone who is content being single and a serial dater?" This intriguing question prompted Frank and Jean to explain their similarities and differences in relationship and marital issues.

In an effort to bridge that gap, Frank and Jean brought on their business partner, Jickael Bazin, who had been divorced for quite some time but was dating again. Jickael's relationship journey made his opinion and advice extremely valuable, because he had experienced what it's like to be deeply in love and then have it ~~have it~~ fall apart. His joy of being married, his pain of being divorce, and what he learned on his road to recovery provided major insight for both Frank and Jean, and an interesting counterpoint to their experiences and opinions. Together, they had something to share, and realizing that their experiences were similar to other men, they wanted to prove to women everywhere that, believe it or not, men do want to find that perfect life-long partner.

Frank, Jean, and Jickael made it their mission to obtain valuable insights from other men, needed information that would add on to their already-growing relationship data, and with no time to waste, they created a survey for single, married, and divorced men; soon afterward, thousands of answered surveys were received. Frank, Jean, and Jickael were astonished that their project—to explore the psyche of single, married, and divorced men—was being realized, but somehow, the resulting blueprint was a tad bit sketchy.

To further add clarity to what was to become the complete SMMM guidebook, Frank, Jean, and Jickael brought on Rae Holliday, a celebrity media personality/expert blogger; Zangba Thomson, a writer and creative director, who previously worked alongside Jean Alerte on *Do Right, Do Good* (a self-help book about vision fulfillment and entrepreneurship); Kel Spencer, an emerging hip-hop artist and award-winning songwriter/warrior poet; and Pervis Taylor, III, a life coach and author of *Pervis Principles Volume 1* and *2*. All of the names mentioned above contributed to the project by adding amazing insights from their fields of expertise. Together, they inadvertently created the "Man Bible" for relationships, a sincere collection that contains the great answer to—Every Man Wants to Get Married, So Why Not to You?

PROLOGUE

BY

ZANGBA THOMSON

Every man wants to get married, so why not to you? Have you ever been in a failed relationship and decided that you will never give your all to anyone ever again? Or are you in a troubling relationship, and every second of the day, you are wondering why your man doesn't acknowledge you like he used to? Men are unpredictable creatures. Many of them lose interest in the objects of their affection—when those people don't look interesting enough to them anymore. The thought of that happening to you scares you to the core, doesn't it? So now you might be thinking, *Does my man find me interesting?* To answer this intriguing question, you may start spending more time than you normally would in front of a mirror. But what exactly is it you are looking for? Clues? Yes, clues that will explain why it's your fault that your man isn't giving you the time of day or the love at night. Then, all of a sudden, your mind begins to play tricks on you. The mirror reveals that you're not pretty anymore. Oh! The excess weight that you are carrying around your waist might be the reason why your man isn't interested. Ouch! But wait, there's another vision popping into your head—maybe there's another woman. Aha! Yes! That's it! It's another woman. You cover your mouth. The fear of losing your man causes you to withdraw into a dark and gloomy place filled with past hurts and resentment. But you've been there before, many times—it's the place you go when all seems lost.

> *"When you get into a tight place and everything goes against you, till it seems as though you could not hang on a minute longer, never give up then, for that is just the place and time that the tide will turn."*
> —Harriet Beecher Stowe

Time and time again, you have given the relationship your all, and time and time again, you have watched your efforts go down the drain. The mental strain of trying to but not being noticed is causing you to go insane. Out of nowhere, a sharp pain shoots through your wounded heart, and it's unbearable—so much so that it causes you to shed tears. You are sad. If only someone would've told you the consequences of love. But you know what?

Alfred Lord Tennyson was right when he wrote, "I hold it true, whatever befall; I feel it, when I sorrow most; 'Tis better to have loved and lost than never to have loved at all." Your insanity is justified.

You call your girlfriend, and she rants, "Don't waste your time crying over him, girl! He's not worth it! There are lots of guys who would love to have you by their side. You need to go out there and find you someone new!" It's true what King Solomon said, "In the multitude of words sin is not lacking, but he who restrains his lips is wise." Well, I guess your girlfriend didn't get Solomon's memo, because after telling you to give up on your relationship, she calls your man every undesirable name in the book, even names that are not written down yet, just to paint a villainous picture of your man. This happened all because you allowed it to happen. You begin to question why you called your friend in the first place. The truth is she's been single for a good while now. What good advice could she possibly give you? The phone call ends abruptly, and you find yourself feeling worse than you did before making the phone call. You start to consider the poisonous thoughts that your friend inserted inside your mind, and you say to the woman in the mirror, "Maybe I should just leave and find someone new, someone who will notice and appreciate me for the beautiful person that I am."

You exhale deeply and take a moment to gather your thoughts. "Insanity is doing the same thing over and over again and expecting different results." A cold chill travels down your spine, and then the light finally dawns on you. You realize that you have been going about things all wrong. How could you have been so naïve to not realize something so obvious? With great enthusiasm, you begin to analyze Einstein's quote.

Insanity. But who's insane? Well, of course you are, right? Doing the same thing over and over again. But what are you doing over and over again? Trying to get your man to pay attention to you, trying to get him to love you more. Or maybe it's just that you want the two of you to communicate more effectively. It's always more, more, and more; you want more out of him and more out of your relationship. When more isn't received, you feel betrayed and assume the worse. Maybe more is something he can't provide at the moment, because the more time he spends working in the world, the more time the world requires of him. Everything is give and take. Whatever you are doing to get his attention isn't working, but still you expect different results than the ones you are getting. So what now? Why not try something different?

If it's not broken, don't fix it, but if it's not working, then something needs to be fixed. What exactly needs to be fixed? The relationship? Maybe it's your man. Maybe it's you. Maybe you need to change in order for your relationship to prosper. You've tried and have given it your all. But are you sure about that? Can you truthfully say that there's nothing more you can do to save your relationship? Maybe your approach to the situation is wrong. Maybe if you tweak things a little, your relationship could change for the better. But the question is: Are you willing to do that? Are you prepared to change how you treat your man?

Sometimes you might see a mirage and think it's real. You might assume your man is cheating because he's too exhausted to communicate or make love to you. Your plight is understood, but your assessment of the situation might not be accurate. Michael Jackson said, "You are not alone," and I say, "Help has arrived." The solution has landed in the form of seven distinguished gentlemen (three single, two married, one divorced, one engaged)

Our purpose is to guide you back to where you belong, in your man's arms—you know, the warm and cozy place that makes you feel safe from harm. For far too long now, you have tried things your way and may have failed. Your trial-and-error approach has caused you to lose hope altogether. You have been seeing things from a female's point of view, but now it's time to look at your situation from a male's perspective. These experiences, which will soon be shared with you, should be classified as priceless to those who want to love and be loved. You are a child of love and it's not by coincidence that you are reading this guidebook.

As you begin to read through the chapters, you will feel yourself becoming free—free from the fear that once weeded your mind with negative thoughts that lead you to make unwise relationship decisions. You will begin to connect the dots. The truth, after it is exposed, will set you free, but it is up to you to comprehend that truth before it sinks back into the pages. You chose this book because you wanted change—change from unhappiness, change from your stressful relationship, and change from disappointments. I say the time is ripe for healing. Forgiveness has found its way into your heart. Embrace it. Open your mind and know that you are responsible for your own happiness and unhappiness.

Single Man, Married Man

Married Man

Every Man Wants to Get Married - Why Not to You?

1

WHY ARE YOU AFRAID TO STROKE HIS EGO?

FRANK GATEAU

"The taste for glory can make ordinary men behave in extraordinary ways."

—Tahir Shah

The best thing that a woman can do in a relationship is stroke her man's ego, which, I must say, needs stroking—all the time. But the stroking must be handled with great care because a man's ego is delicate.

In a relationship, a man's goal is to protect and provide security for his woman. Pleasing her is high on his list, but if he feels he can't satisfy her, or if his relationship with her becomes too much of a hassle, then he will not hesitate to leave the relationship and move on. His woman must allow him to lead and take control. She must have faith in him, and she shouldn't be afraid to tell him how good he makes her feel. She should take pride in the things that he has accomplished and compliment him on them.

But nowadays, women feel that if they stroke their man's ego, it will give him an inflated sense of confidence. Well, yeah—that's the point. A woman who strokes her man's ego will definitely benefit across the board. And if you need to know one thing about your man, you should know that stroking his ego is the driving force behind his success.

Ego stroking shouldn't be viewed as a competition, because it isn't, and contrary to what some women believe, ego stroking doesn't make a man feel superior to his woman. No. Ego stroking strengthens the man and makes him feel confident to a point where he feels powerful enough to *want* to take better care of his woman.

The fight is not in the relationship; it's with the outside world. The stronger a female can make me feel, the stronger our relationship will be. Men need to feel appreciated and needed, and stroking our ego is critical in sustaining a quality relationship with us. So, to all the women out there in the world who are struggling to keep their relationships afloat, learn ego stroking today, develop it, and apply it in your relationship. Over the course of time, you will see your relationship improve.

The time spent with your man will get better. Conversations will be enjoyable and will end in laughter, instead of useless bickering. Instead of only getting gifts on Christmas and birthdays, you will be showered with gifts regularly—because you were wise enough to show appreciation for the things he does for you. But not stroking your man's ego is a sign of insecurity, and I can honestly say that I had longer relationships with women who stroked my ego. Ego stroking obviously isn't the only component in making a relationship work, but it's very important, because you will become more attractive to your man. He will see you in a different light. It's the simple things in life that make a difference.

So are you ready to bare yourself to him? Are you ready to stroke his ego by letting go of yours? I can't speak for every man, but I love compliments. A kind word, a smile, or a simple gesture can go a long way. If he smells good, tell him! He's looking good in his attire? Tell him! He's turning you on? Tell him! Stop being afraid to let him know that you really like him. In today's world, some independent women feel that they don't need a man for anything. They feel they can do *A* to *Z* all by themselves, and believe me, many of them can. But being too self-sufficient can become problematic when trying to secure a long-term relationship.

Most men, including myself, shy away from women who have "I don't need a man for anything" syndrome. Some of these women's biggest complaints when searching for a partner are: he lacks ambition; he's too complacent with mediocrity; he can't do anything for me that I can't do for myself. So when you find your-self a man with drive and ambition, someone who gets the job done, don't forget to praise him for what he's worth—especially since you claim these types of men are so scarce. Stop forcing them away. Stroke his ego. Be his biggest cheerleader. Learn about his interests and show him that you are interested. Tell him how remarkable he is. It's no secret: if you give, you shall receive.

Even the R&B girl group Destiny's Child showed they knew about this with their song "Cater 2 U." They knew that no matter where a woman was in life, she should always be able to cater to her man's needs—prepare his meals, draw him a bath, and massage his feet every now and then. "Cater 2 U" should be on every woman's playl-ist and kept on repeat.

Try not to bombard your man with unnecessary questions as soon as he gets home. Just give him a hug. Allow him to unwind from a long day at work. Walk up to him and say, "Baby, you look like you had a long day.

Is there anything I can get for you to make you feel more comfortable?" Watch how quickly his tail will start wagging like a happy dog's ("dog" being used only as a figure of speech here).

I used to date a girl, and every time "Cater 2 U" came on the radio, she would get this repulsive look on her face and attempt to change the station. (Note: Changing the station, especially if we're in my vehicle is a major no-no.) Even though she jokingly played it off, her actions represented how she actually felt, and our relationship didn't last long because she didn't understand how to cater to the needs of the relationship. She didn't know that ego stroking could've done wonders for our relationship. But that's neither here nor there; I used that example to say this—you should always make your man feel like he's president of the United States of America. When he says something funny, smile because he loves to see that he makes you smile. He might not be funny as Kevin Hart, Will Ferrell, or Eddie Murphy, but reassure him that he's funny in his own way. Even if a joke isn't funny, guess what? You should still laugh! Laugh at the fact that it isn't funny. When he feels appreciated, he will go out of his way to treat you like the queen that you are becoming. Make him feel like he's number one by stroking his ego. Don't just say it. Show it. Action speaks volumes louder than words can ever do.

I can practically hear women right now—both married women who are in dysfunctional relationships and single women who can't keep the right man—yelling, "Yeah right! Picture me stroking his ego! He should be catering to me!" If you think it's all about you, you are absolutely right, because *you* will be the only person you have to call your own.

RAE HOLLIDAY

When it comes to the males of the species, there isn't a single man on planet Earth who doesn't want his ego stroked. Are you willing to do that for your man? Many times, women who are recuperating from failed relationships let their negative experiences settle into their DNA. They put up a wall or make a mental note to not stroke anyone's ego because they don't want anyone to become too controlling or have more control over them.

The key is not to enter into a new relationship with your old relationship still fresh in your mind. Every new relationship deserves its own foundation, and a new set of rules needs to be established. Each moment should come with a clean slate. If the slate isn't clean, things could get really shambolic. You really have to wing it and give your new partner the benefit of the doubt, knowing that everything happens for a reason.

Relationships are all about compromise. When both parties realize something or come to a mutual agreement, then the relationship can move forward and blossom. So learn to play your part and don't be afraid to stroke your man's ego. The result will be a fulfilling relationship with many magical moments.

JICKAEL BAZIN

Your man is an ego-driven creature, so every now and then; you have to stroke his ego. This unselfish act will feed his confidence, which allows him to be the man in the relationship, and in its simplest form, it is your way of letting him know that he is doing a great job.

"You never know when a moment and a few sincere words can have an impact on a life."
—Zig Ziglar

One of the biggest ways to stroke your man's ego is through communication. You have to talk the talk before you can walk the walk. I personally enjoy the deep and meaningful conversations I have with my female companions. It's amazing what you can learn about someone when you engage in conversations that lead from one great topic to another. But this conversational utopia only occurs when couples are in a state of peace and harmony, when both parties feel confident knowing that they can relate on many different topics, including personal and social ones. When a man feels that he is able to connect with his woman, this becomes food for his ego.

Communication is equally as important when things aren't going well. Your man notices when you have a frown on your face, when the world has offended you, and when you retreat to that lonely place where you feel safe, far behind the elusive wall that comes up whenever you feel threatened. "What's wrong, babe?" he might ask you.

"Nothing!" you might reply emotionally, your answer like fingernails on a chalkboard.

Your man only wants to protect you, but you won't let him. "What's wrong?" he asks again, determined to find out what's going on. Hopefully, he can find a way to put that beautiful smile back on your endearing face.

"I had a horrible day at work," you finally say, breaking out of your shell and allowing him to become the hero during your great dilemma. He might not be able to fix your problem right away, but he might brighten your day by making you see things in a different light, from a more positive vantage point. By allowing your man to assist you in your time of need, you have made him feel good, and this good feeling feeds his ego.

Whether in private or public, it's crucial not to overlook stroking your man's ego. When you bring him around your friends and family, remember to treat him well. It's important to him that your family and friends see him as someone who can protect and provide for you, and a direct reflection of that is how you treat him around them. When introducing him to your friends and family, mention how you admire him or why you are in love with him. If he is relatively new to your family, don't leave him on his own for too long; he will get restless and not want to be there. So every now and then, pass by and say, "Hey, babe. I'm just checking on you. Can I get you anything?" If you two are going through a turbulent time, never point out his flaws in front of your friends and family. This is a definite don't-do. Airing out his dirty laundry in public is a sure way to bruise his ego, and a bruised ego sows seeds of resentment that may lay dormant and eventually cause harm to your relationship in the future.

If your man is able to meet 70–80 percent of your needs, then stroking his ego should come naturally. Don't feel as if stroking his ego will cause him to stop doing certain things. On the contrary, when he gets his ego stroked, he will be more inclined to love you more. Stroking a man's ego is like an adrenaline rush that explodes and adds growth to your relationship.

DR. JEAN ALERTE

"...we must go beyond the constant clamor of ego, beyond the tools of logic and reason, to the still, calm place within us: the realm of the soul."
—Deepak Chopra

Ego could stand for "Every man Got One." But what exactly does "one" mean in that sense? One woman to marry? One life to live? Or better yet, one destiny to fulfill? The benefit of ego stroking is mutual. Both sides are happy, and there's no room to complain because everyone's ego is being stroked.

The emotional complexities of women vary; some are afraid, and others are not, both for a multitude of reasons. Certainly everyone should give credit where credit is due, but unfortunately, some of us are so egotistical that it's impossible to give attention and appreciation to others who deserve gratitude. Sometimes we don't see the wisdom in stroking our mate's ego. Why should a person feel the need to have their ego stroked? Is it because of insecurities or feelings of inadequacy? And whose role is it to check whether someone's ego is healthy and balanced? Proverbs 27:17 states, "As iron sharpens iron, so one person sharpens another." Likewise, while a woman is sharpening her man's ego, he is also sharpening hers. Everything should be reciprocal in a loving relationship.

Take this scenario into consideration. Let's say in elementary school, a boy is having bad experiences talking to girls. At home, his mother doesn't give him any love or affection, so fast-forward into the future; the boy is an adult now, his confidence is nonexistent, and he shies away from communicating with women altogether. No one suspects anything because he's very quiet and keeps to himself. His insecurities are never analyzed, and he carries them with him into a new relationship. For argument's sake, let's say this new relationship he has is with you. All is well while the emotional flood of admiration continues to pour, but once that appreciation stops or a problem arises, he breaks down systematically, because he doesn't know how to communicate effectively due to his lack of confidence with women. That's when the art of ego stroking comes into play. That's when the magic begins to transpire.

When you stroke your man's ego time and time again, giving him that jump-start that every man needs, you will see his confidence begin to soar. It will reach new heights, and suddenly your man will feel comfortable opening up to you—all because you stroked his ego, because you made him feel special. All along, you thought he was conservative and low-key, but you have now found out that he's funny and charismatic. That's the power of ego stroking; it can transform a person's life forever.

The lesson is this: once couples understand each other's insecurities, the dynamics of their relationship will change for the better and love will flow naturally. Both people can work together to find a wholeness that will meet their individual needs. Emotional dependencies must be acknowledged, and a commitment to improving these insecurities must be agreed upon. You must consistently work toward betterment to achieve growth and healing. We have to remember that fear is based on thoughts about things that may or may not even happen in the future. We should never let our fears determine our choices. Life is about living; there is no future in fear. Don't allow fear of the unknown to create a breakdown in communication. Make it your business, your goal, to make your man feel loved and appreciated. The results will be fulfilling. Always give, because the love you withhold is rooted in the pain that you carry. It takes a happy couple to create a village that can nurture and raise a family. So treat each other like royalty.

KEL SPENCER

"Part of me suspects that I'm a loser, and the other part of me thinks I'm God Almighty."
—John Lennon

I remember getting out of his car. I slammed the door and walked into the lobby of the Beverly Garland Hotel in Studio City, Los Angeles. But before he drove off, he rolled his window down and screamed, "Matter of fact, I'll pick you up at ten instead of eleven tomorrow morning!"

"A'ight, bet!" I responded, before walking up to my room with mixed feelings. The year was 2000. It was my first trip to L.A., and I was there working on my first writing project—the *Wild Wild West* soundtrack. During the session, it was brought to my attention that my own album would be put on hold. But while I was waiting, there were two other well-known artists who wanted me to do some writing for their projects. As awesome of an opportunity as it was, the first thing that came to my mind was, *How will people know that I wrote it?* Pretty selfish, huh? I spoke to my father about it, and I explained all of the angles that I could see.

He listened quietly on the other end of the phone, and once I was done talking, he simply said, "Humility is doing the work and not needing the credit for it." I was frozen by his response, namely because, at that time, I had just started reading the Bible. I was at that late teenage/early twenties crossroad, where I wanted to mature, and the Bible was the route I chose. In my reading and studying, humility came up a lot. I later learned that I would get full credit for all of my writing and that it would be a pretty enriching experience overall.

You see, your reputation is what others think of you. Your ego is what you think of yourself. Both are rooted in valid reasoning, but neither is necessarily the truth, and reputation and ego don't always match. It takes humility to realize this. It also takes humility to manage them both. The gentleman in the car at the hotel was Omarr Rambert. At the time, he was my A&R, my mentor, a big brother, and probably the most influential person in my overall development in the entertainment business. But before we got to that point, about a year earlier, we had met in a studio in Philadelphia called A Touch of Jazz. It was Jazzy Jeff's studio, and the first thing I had to do was rap. I must've done about thirty different rhymes in front of this guy, and the whole time, he had sat there with a straight face, eating a cheesesteak. I wasn't used to that type of response, or shall I say nonresponse. That situation was an ego killer. I went from shows and demos, to being the big man on Morgan State's campus, to attracting this big meeting, to possibly signing with a major label, to getting the straight face. Omarr then walked me down the hallway and around the corner, to a room in the back. When the door opened, Jazzy Jeff was sitting there looking through crates of records. Omarr looked at Jeff and finally broke his composure. "Yo, Jeff," he said. "This is Kel. Throw on a beat. This dude can spit!"

Those were two of many experiences in which my reputation didn't mean a whole lot at that moment in time. Those were two situations in which, if I had been married or in a committed relationship, the worst thing that I could've received from my woman would have been a cold and stiff understanding of what I was feeling. It's in those moments that men need their egos repaired. We don't need to be lied to. We don't need to be puffed up and worshiped. But in the midst of working on humility, at times, we need our woman's words to be the brick and mortar that rebuild our egos—in a healthy way, not in the form of pedestal placement.

So don't be afraid to stroke your man's ego. It's not that he needs to feel like a god. It's not that he needs to feel like Superman. But in a world where this internal conflict between reputation and ego rages and it isn't something that's readily talked about, whatever reassurance escapes from your lips will most likely be exactly what your man needs at any given moment. And if there is an internal conflict going on, why don't you both talk about it? In Genesis, God spoke life into existence, so you can also speak beautiful words to resuscitate your man's wounded ego—especially when it is on the verge of annihilation. Your man's reputation may or may not fuel his ego, but his ego will most likely fuel his choices, and his choices will determine his success and, sometimes, failures. You don't have to stroke your man's ego every day, but you do have to stroke it every now and then. Your man needs the confidence of his other half—sometimes better half—to come in the form of an ego booster. So don't be afraid to stroke his ego.

Life Coach Note
by Pervis Taylor

The ego is very powerful, and a man's ego is super fragile. It's important to note that men need to be affirmed just as much as women do. I always tell women you will get more out of your man if you empower him in his position as the head and leader of your relationship. The reality is more often than not that his ego is getting crushed at work, and today's media and culture has a way of depreciating men's role in society. The last place where he wants to feel devalued is in the home and in his relationship. Chris Burge says "men scream at a frequency that only they can hear." Men are comfortable displaying two emotions: anger and indifference. If you can create a space where your man feels safe, he will open his heart to you. But as with everything in life, it is a process. The first step is to empower your man. Make him feel desired, treasured, and needed. I know, for some women, this seems like an exercise in futility. However, if you are willing to be different, you will get a different result out of your man. Moreover, if you learn to study him, you'll know when and how you need to empower him. More often than not, it's the timing of when things are done. I've counseled couples where the woman did empower her man, but the timing was always off. Maybe she tried to stroke his ego when things were good (which is needed), but when he was down, she pried about the source of his hurt. In the past, I have suggested women give their men a bit of a space, to let them process, and then when their men are ready, the women can offer their encouragement and ego stroke. Men are emotionally fragile; we are just good at hiding it. There is no one in the world who doesn't need to be affirmed. I've counseled couples where the woman withheld her praise from her husband because she was so angry and wanted to hurt him. Thus, the relationship began to dissolve. Our words create our world, and believe it or not, they create the worlds of others in our lives. Ladies, if you want to have a beautiful, lasting relationship with your significant other, be extremely generous with your words of encouragement and love.

2

ARE YOU PREPARED FOR HIS LOVE?

FRANK GATEAU

I am ready to give 100 percent to the woman I choose to be involved with if I see long-term potential. I'm prepared to keep it real, and from the beginning, I will let her know what my intentions are. I've dated a lot of women who didn't have any long-term goals, and because they were short-term thinkers, our relationships didn't work. But when I find a woman who truly compliments me, I will be that good man that she's been looking for.

But in order to be loved, you must first love you. A lot of single women nowadays are looking for love, but they are not mentally ready for the challenge of finding true love. First and foremost, a woman must have an open mind, minus all the negative preconceptions of her past, before entering into a brand-new relationship. She must dispose of all the negative energy from her previous relationships. Remember that every man is innocent until proven guilty, not the other way around.

Several men and women have a fear of being alone, and for women, this negative emotion causes them to settle fast with someone new before fully healing from their previously failed relationships. But having one foot in the past and one in the present leads to disaster. I see it all the time—a woman mentally stuck in the past while her new "bae" is doing everything in his power to make her happy. But it's a waste of his time because he is with a woman who is still stuck in her past relationship. For things to work, she must move on from the past, realize her true value, and take her time before running into and onto the next person.

Time and people are two things you shouldn't take for granted. Learn from your mistakes, and don't waste your time trying to change your man. Spend that time changing yourself for the better. I always hear single women saying, "I'm looking for a good man," but unfortunately, half of the women saying that don't project themselves as good women. Please don't be that type! You are a reflection of the type of person you attract! You should realize that a good man would not keep a dreadful woman.

I am a visual creature, and looking, smelling, and touching arouse me, so however a woman displays herself in public, whether it is looking sexy or acting fast and "free," I will judge her based on her behavior and appearance. Her public presentation is key. Don't get me wrong; women should feel free to express and display themselves however they feel. We love that, but be conscious of the message you're putting out there, especially if the reaction you're getting from men isn't what you're looking for. Sure, it will intrigue us to test-drive the product, but it doesn't guarantee that we'll want to purchase it.

Some women have the habit of hiding their emotions and feelings because, if they reveal them, they feel they will get hurt. But I don't agree with that way of thinking. I feel if more women displayed their true emotions and feelings, their relationships would last longer. Their relationships probably won't be free from problems, and no one should expect their relationships to be. No relationship in life is, but at least everything will be out in the open. Transparency is best. But if a woman's feelings are held in, she is only suppressing the essence of what makes her a woman, and her relationship will suffer.

Ladies, if you don't open up, then all your fears and insecurities will disrupt what you have. Don't let fear stop you from saying what you genuinely feel. Express yourself.

I understand that some women are juggling their careers and personal life. I don't have a problem with that. My issue is that you shouldn't let it consume you to a point where you are not able to love or be loved by your man. If your busyness is not allowing him to love you effectively, guess what? There's an abundance of single women out there who will catch his eye. Remember, men have a short attention span.

"Forgive the past. It is over. Learn from it and let go. People are constantly changing and growing. Do not cling to a limited, disconnected, negative image of a person in the past."
—Brian Weiss

Think like an athlete if nothing else. Sportspeople know what it takes to win. They are constantly in training, preparing to be the best in their respective fields. They perform when they are healthy or injured. To them, the pain doesn't matter because their mind is focused on attaining the prize.

They know how to receive advice and criticism. What's the one thing that all of the greatest athletes in the world have in common? They all had a coach. From Michael Jordan to Kobe Bryant, to LeBron James, they all had great coaches in their lives who were able to help them achieve greatness. These coaches were nowhere near as good of players as these athletes were, but they were able to see the game from the outside looking in, and from this viewpoint, they were able to show their superstars what they were doing right, what they were doing wrong, and how they could elevate their game to the next level.

There are lots of similarities between a sports team and a couple in a relationship. The team plays through their winning and losing streaks, while the couple tries their best to love each other through good and bad times. But it's how an athlete responds and comes back from adversity when their true character is revealed. Are you someone who folds under pressure? Or are you the persevering type? Will you quit on your man when your situation changes for the worse? Or will you stand your ground, knowing that one day the storm will blow over? Generation X tends to quit as soon as there is some type of adversity. It's easy to pack up and leave, but when you work hard to make your relationship work, you will appreciate it a little more and fight to make it last.

A person's true character is always shown when they are under pressure. Winners don't make excuses. They go out there and get the job done. Are you willing to do that? Or will you let your busy schedule dictate your life, dictate your home, dictate your future?

Remember, you don't have to be perfect; just try to be the best you that you can be, and no matter what, you should always feel happy and secure. The key is to find out what makes you happy and then find someone you can share that happiness with. Men can always tell that something is wrong when a woman needs a man to make her feel special. If you are looking for a man to complete you, then you are not prepared for his love. To begin with, if you are not whole within, then your relationship will be incomplete as well. Focus on your interest, and do what makes you happy. When you are happy, then you are ready.

Understand that the dynamics of your past relationships can have major consequences on your present and future relationships. Women who like to keep close ties with their exes need to be cautious because it's mind-boggling hearing a woman criticize her exes but then turn around and say "we're still close friends." If these exes are so bad, why do these women still choose to remain friends with them? When their new guy questions them about it, they get accused of being jealous. But if the shoe were on the other foot, would they feel the same way? If children aren't involved, then I don't see any reason why a woman should feel the need to remain close friends with her ex. That puts a strain on her new relationship.

Is your mail still being delivered to your ex's address? If so, go to the post office and request an address change. You and him shared a family plan on your phones, and now your relationship is over? Well, that line is now dead; it's time to update your plan! You have to move on—not just physically, but with everything else also. Maybe it will cost you a few bucks more to get your own line, but so what? Through your friends and family, he might know about your whereabouts. Well, guess what? Inform them that you two are no longer together and that they definitely shouldn't be releasing any information about you to him. If he was your best friend, then maybe you should stay with him, instead of moving on to the next guy. In order to build trust with your new person, you need to leave the old one in the past.

Think positive. Don't go around saying, "There aren't any good men out here!" or, "Men only want one thing!" Be careful with what you say because the energy you put out there will be the energy you receive. For so long, you've been meeting bad guys, guys who only want you for sex. For so long, you've been saying, "Men are dogs!" What did you expect? And why haven't you noticed that the words coming out of your mouth are shaping your reality? Why not say, "I will find a good man, and he will love me for who I am"? Be optimistic. Speak health into your life, and refrain from speaking ill about yourself and others.

Ultimately, you have to make some adjustments. Learn to accept your man for who he is, appreciate him, try to understand him, and let him know that he makes you happy. Put down your defensive shield. Open up. Be receptive but have confidence in yourself. Don't be afraid to be vulnerable. Have a strong sense of respect for yourself and him. Show him why you are deserving. Be eager to listen and be open to suggestions. Be willing to try new things. Men and women feel the same emotions when it comes to love, but it is the journey that is experienced differently. Show your man the best version of you. By this, I don't mean putting on makeup or dressing up in high heels (even though it's necessary to take pride in your appearance and hygiene). What I'm talking about is having an unlocked personality. Be more appealing from within, and your outside will naturally look good. Be considerate. Help him without him having to ask you for help. The smallest gestures make the biggest impressions. If you can help it, don't bring any negativity around him. Focus on what's right and not on what's wrong. Positivity breeds more positivity. I'm not saying that you have to agree with everything your man is saying, or you shouldn't have complaints, because everyone does. You should express yourself, but don't just constantly gripe about things. Have faith and try to find an approach that will help alleviate the problem.

Never try to force a situation. What is meant to be will be. Eventually, someone will come along. Timing is important. The right person could be sitting right next to you and you don't even know it. You and him might constantly be crossing paths, and you don't even notice because you are too busy thinking, *There are no good men out there.* If that is the case, you need to adjust your ill way of thinking, because it has caused you much unhappiness.

Me, personally, I want a God-fearing woman, someone who will motivate me to become a better person; a woman who has a good sense of humor, someone who likes to enjoy life, loves being spontaneous and adventurous; someone fun, alive, and vibrant; a woman who knows what she wants and isn't afraid to let me know it. I hate surprises, and I don't like being caught off guard with complex questions. I want my woman to keep it simple. She has to know her worth, and she must possess self-respect. She must be able to carry and present herself in a respectful manner, someone who doesn't feel the need to go out there and be seen, and someone who can get attention without begging for it. She doesn't have to be in the spotlight all the time. Sometimes women get too comfortable around their man in the early stages. I'm sorry, but farting, burping loudly, and cursing like winos do in dark alleyways is unacceptable. A woman should never forget that she is a woman, and in a way, a woman falls from grace when her man sees her acting in this rude and belligerent way. So please, act ladylike, gentle, and nurturing. Being this way shows that you respect yourself first and foremost. I had a friend, and we were exploring the idea of dating. Needless to say, she was very comfortable around me. She would burp and pass gas, and she even took it a step further and made jokes about the stench in the room. But what part of the game was that? It's a natural human function, but be considerate about it when you are dating. Don't lose touch with your feminine side. Be a lady, and your man will love you for that. Avoid being a drama queen, and be known as a woman who provides her man with peace of mind.

RAE HOLLIDAY

Love is an action verb, and therefore, sweating is required in order to fulfill it. There's no way you can tell someone that you love him or her without showing him or her love. In a relationship, *love* is many people's favorite word because they know once they tell their mate "I love you" that they will get what they want. So unfortunately, a lot of men use the word *love* to get what they want. Is it right?

Of course not; it's definitely wrong. But what a woman needs to ask is this—am I prepared to love and be loved?

Once you get passed the mind games and saying "I love you" just to be saying it; once you get serious about your relationship and start putting action behind your words, it means that you are ready for his love. But are you ready to receive everything that you think you want? The idea of being in love is amazing, but love comes with its ups and downs. Your love could be good one day and bad the next. Love can also depend on family. Sometimes family has a lot to do with it. Are you ready to incorporate their love into your relationship? You see, love never shows up without a suitcase or two; relationships can always bring extra baggage. At the end of the day, will you be packing or unpacking? Being ready for love is a real challenge. Will you pass or fail? These are the types of questions you need to answer because women who overcome this test are ready to get married.

JICKAEL BAZIN

I am fully capable of falling in love, and when I do, it's deep. This may be the main reason why I guard my heart and emotions. A natural human law is to avoid pain, and I believe society has molded me to believe that if I want to avoid pain, I shouldn't express my true senti-ments. So I walk around all day long with a poker face. My attitude is to never let them see me sweat, but behind my stony expression is a loving man who is looking for love.

Growing up, my parents showed me lots of love but hardly ever told me that they loved me. So I grew up thinking that's how life is—you can show love, but don't you dare say it out loud.

In *Love & Other Drugs*, a movie about a young woman suffering from Parkinson's disease, there was a segment where Jake Gyllenhaal's character, Jamie Randall, tried to tell Anne Hathaway's character, Maggie Murdock, that he loves her. He was so stricken by his emotions, and by the fact that he had never uttered "I love you" to any-one before, nor had anyone ever said those lovely words to him, that he hyperventilates uncontrollably simply because he is about to say it. Although the movie is fic-tional, Jamie's reaction to saying "I love you" is not far from how I feel. But why do I feel this way? Is it because I have been hurt before, so severely that I go out of my way to avoid being in a relationship? Subconsciously, the fear of being in that vulnerable state terrifies me to a point where I'm content with being single. However, I want to fall in love again. I want to love and be loved again. But how can I find love if I'm off the dating radar?

Is it possible that a man with a heart as strong as mine has had it broken so deeply that avoiding the reoccurrence of such pain has completely closed it to the possibilities of ever feeling love again? However, how can I ever find love again if I don't leave my heart open enough to even see the possibilities?

You see love is a two-way street and Cupid is always on his job. There's nowhere to run, nowhere to hide, because love is inevitable. The overwhelming majority of us will feel love sooner or later—for the first time or again and again until we get it right. Love is one of the basic human needs. Everyone needs to love and be loved. But the question is—what will you do when love finds you? Will you be ready for it?

I know there are a lot of woman out there who want to be in a loving relationship. Do not despair, but ask yourself, "What will I do once love has entered into my life?" Will you be able to sincerely tell your partner "I love you"? If you are reluctant in expressing those words, you are probably simply trying to avoid pain; the first time you get your heart broken can be catastrophic.

Although studies show that most men predominately have sex on their minds, more often than not, I do not. I am often thinking of ways to simply put a smile on my partner's face.

I know we all have similar needs. We may have different goals, values, and morals, but the basic human needs are consistent; the need for certainty, the need to feel comfortable, the need to avoid pain and gain pleasure, the need for surprises and for challenges, and the need to feel significant, to feel like we matter, to feel unique in some way, to feel needed and more. These needs are what make life exciting, but how do you go about meeting them?

> *"You must realize that you have to look at your marriage and understand what is needed in your marriage, not what people think your marriage should be, not what people want your marriage to be, but you have to both look at each other and see what you need as individuals and then look at the union and see what the union needs and make decisions based on that, not based on what people think marriage should be."*
> —Jada Pinkett Smith

Relationships are all about meeting each other's needs. If your man makes you feel comfortable and secure; helps you experience more variety, like learning new things and challenging your intellect; if he makes you feel special and unique to a point where you value him and see his unique qualities; if you can connect and relate; if all these things are so, then you should appreciate him and acknowledge him so that he feels it. Connect with him mentally, physically, and emotionally. The more you do, the more you and he will grow. Hopefully, your relationship was developed in rich soil, and the fertilizer called love is nurturing you and your man's planted seeds. Day by day, you and your man have grown. But to make your relationship relevant, you both must be continuously ready for each other's love. Because if his needs aren't being met, then guess what? Yours won't either. You won't feel loved because he isn't being loved by you, and you won't feel special because you aren't treating him special. You won't feel appreciated because he feels underappreciated. These are signs you will notice when things are beginning to fall apart.

Love is a need so deep within us that it is a survival instinct. That's how important it is. The best way to create a great relationship is to first create a great relationship with yourself. If you go into a relationship to be loved and do not give love back in return, then you are setting yourself up for a lackluster situation. You can't go into a relationship with an empty gallon and expect to fill someone else's up. All that you are looking for is already inside of you, so ask yourself, "What's worth loving about me?"

DR. JEAN ALERTE

Are you willing to bow out of the dating game? Are you ready to settle down with the man of your dreams? The women I asked these two questions to answered, "Yes I am! But, Jean, the real question is, is he prepared for my love?" They were all, I assume, being genuine, but I know from experience, everyone that says, yes doesn't mean yes deep down in their hearts. They are only saying yes because they think it's the answer that will get them what they want. Now, don't get me wrong. Deep down, they might genuinely think saying, "Yes, I am ready to settle down," is the truth, but could it be an unrealistic truth?

If you are still making the mistake of catering to your past, then you are not prepared for the future. You have to take every situation as a new opportunity. Of course you learned lessons from previous relationships, but you have to understand that there's a time in everyone's life when they have to move on. Everything in life is either a lesson or a blessing, so be thankful for both because that's how you grow. Learning and adapting to your new situation is a difficult task, so don't make it even more difficult than it has to be. Maintaining a healthy relationship is a lot of hard work and can become exasperating at times. However, the benefits of a healthy relationship emotionally, spiritually, physically, and financially will always outweigh any obstacles. It's very important to create a balance between the man and woman. All areas are equally important, and one area should not overshadow another.

So are you prepared to love and be loved? I know you've been waiting, and it may feel like it's been an eternity that you've waited for your true love to surface. Are you ready to see your lover as your soul mate and not your adversary? Will you allow him to be on the same team as you? Can the two of you tackle your challenges together as a unit? Can you explore your dreams together? In your heart, can you honestly say that you are not complete without your man? To you, does the LOVE stand for: Living One's Vibrational Energy? And if so, are you prepared to love responsibly? Can you sustain your man in his times of need? When he is weak, can you be strong and uplift his spirit? Can you feed him spiritually, emotionally, and physically? Will he be able to feel your love? Can you work out any troubles with him that come your way and overcome them together?

Sometimes, the things of the world can wreak havoc and put pressure on people's relationships, but don't let that happen to yours. Be diligent. Be forever on the lookout for distractions that are trying to separate you from your man. The word around town is, most relationships fail because of deficiencies in finances, sex, and communication. The need to acquire material things can create barriers that inhibit your spirit from rising to its fullest potential; therefore, you must stay focused on your higher and positive energies and block the thoughts of the lower negative energies. Two incomes amount to more than one, two minds are more creative than one, and two bodies are more capable than one. Love needs nourishment like a flower needs water. All your desires come in God's timing. Remember there is a blessing in the pressing.

KEL SPENCER

"When the student is ready the teacher will appear"
~Ancient Proverb

Contrary to popular opinion, Love is actually not an emotion. It's a choice. Love has emotions that come with it but it's the choice to give to another at the expense of self. "God so Loved the world that he gave..." If Love was an emotion you'd always *feel* it when you love someone yet, we can agree that there are some people we can't stand at times but we still love them, and we do so by way of choice.

In contrast, (No offense to Radio Raheem from the Spike Lee Joint "**Do The Right Thing**" the opposite of Love is not Hate. The opposite of Love is Lust. While Love is the desire to please another at the expense of self, Lust is the desire to please self at the expense of others. Just as there are different types of Lust (ie for power, for money, for sex, etc...) based on the emotion attached, there are also different types of Love based on the emotion attached.

As English speakers, often times our concept of love is limited because we only have one word for love. Whereas the Greek language has different words for different types of love. Phileos for example, is the love for your brother or close friend. This is where we get Philadelphia, the city of brotherly love. This is why I don't have the same love for my brothers that I do for my fiancé, and I don't have the same love for my Grandmother that I do for my car.

Why am I getting this deep into love? For one simple reason—for you to understand its meaning. I've seen women get butterflies in their stomachs and swoon just because a man said the words, "I love you." But he didn't necessarily show it. He didn't even say that he knew what it meant. But because he used those words, it got him a golden ticket. When I first told my fiancée that I loved her, I gave her the definition first. I then went on to say, "Based on my desire, based on my commitment to that desire, I love you." The definition sets the stage. Most people in a committed relationship use that word as a means to display a high level of romantic attraction. And that's fine. But there is a lot of gray area when using *love* in that regard. If you define *love* and make love the battery of your relationship, then love will save the day. You have to determine if you're ready for a man's love or not. You have to decide if you're ready to live and breathe and have your being within that committed relationship, on a stage that has been set by the definition of love that I just gave you. You can't just accept professed love and experience butterflies and bat your eyelashes, unable to control your increased heart rate, just because a man uttered the *L* word. No. You were pretty much faced with an invisible, intangible, yet very present contract that will require a degree of readiness from you. It is now on you to maintain a certain level of interaction with this man. You are now faced with the task of remaining at a certain level of intelligence, a certain level of spiritual discipline, a certain type of personality, and a certain degree of physical upkeep. You are also faced with a decision to walk away or to commit to this man's decision to commit, which implies that the you that he has committed to cannot stray too far away from itself.

So, I ask you: Are you ready for his love? Are you ready for the love of a man who knows what love is? Are you ready for love from a man who loves to love? You see, Adam was here first, and when Eve was created, the first thing that she was introduced to was a relationship. Therefore, I believe that women are naturally engineered to be in relationship more than men, to be more interactive, more nurturing and caring, and more expressive and better listeners. I do believe that women are internally and emotionally ready, but are they mentally ready? And it's the mind that ultimately makes that choice to be committed or not. Are you ready? Are you prepared for that type of committed love?

I'm a man, and I will do and say things that may appear to be contrary to love. But wanting to be left alone for a little while doesn't mean that I don't love you. Being annoyed at your indecisiveness whenever I ask you what you'd like to eat doesn't mean that I don't love you. My frustration at people outside of our relationship knowing things about our relationship before

I do doesn't mean that I don't love you. I will still love you through those things even though it may not feel like love. That takes mental readiness, so are you ready for that?

Unfortunately, I don't see too many women preparing themselves for love. I don't see too many people doing it in general. But for women to be the most vocal about wanting a good man and/or waiting on the right one, I would think that during the wanting and waiting, they would be busy and focused at Camp Get Ready. But that's not the case. A good man is going to love you the way that I've explained earlier. What are you doing in your single life to prepare for that? What woman have you taken on as a mentor? What relationships do you use as a template? What books have you read about relationships? Which male friend do you use for insight? What are you doing to prepare yourself? Too many women want to be married, but not enough women are ready to become wives. When you focus and prepare for being a virtuous woman, for being a solid example of a wife and a woman who is ready to love and be loved, I believe at that magical moment, your vision will increase, your list of values and deal breakers will be a lot more conducive to your magnetic pull, and your suitable mate shall appear— maybe more than once.

LIFE COACH NOTE
by Pervis Taylor

Love is a choice. Receiving love is an even more power-ful choice. Often, our inability to receive love is directly related to our concept of love and the love we've expe-rienced—or not experienced. I always tell women who truly desire to have a relationship to seek to have a whole life. Wholeness includes loving ourselves. Jesus was so powerful when he said, "love thy neighbor as thyself." The biggest problem is that a lot of people are incapable of loving and receiving love because they do not love themselves. Seek to fall in love with the person you are, not who you envision yourself to be. Love has a great deal to do with acceptance. Accept who you are and love her. This will help you accept and know what love is or isn't. But I'm going to be honest; most people are afraid to face themselves. It's not easy to truly embrace who we are underneath the veneer that we put on for society. To put it plainly, you want a man to love who you are truly, not just what you represent. But, as I stated, to be pre-pared for a man to love you requires that you undergo the process of truly loving yourself and having your own existence outside of him. Breaking down the falsehoods of what love is will better equip you as well. Love doesn't hurt. Arguing and cursing each other out daily isn't love; it's dysfunction. Relationships are not easy. You're dealing with two broken individuals coming from various experiences that have colored their perspectives on things, love being a prominent one. I tell my clients, "Always do your part." Roll up your sleeves and do the work needed, so you can be loved the way you should be.

3

ARE YOU TOO STRONG, OR IS HE TOO WEAK?

FRANK GATEAU

Nowadays, a lot of women feel that successful, intelligent, and strong women intimidate men. But contrary to that belief, a secure man knows the value in having a strong woman by his side. Trust me, every man wants a strong woman who is confident, someone who knows her place and, at the same time, someone who allows her man to be the man. Are you that woman? Do you act respectfully when getting your point across? Do you know the difference between being aggressive, angry, stubborn, closed off, overly competitive, and strong? If so, then every man wants a woman like you—a woman who can compliment her man and who knows how to back him up in his time of need; someone who isn't overly competitive or, worse-case scenario, someone threatening. As a woman, you must allow your man to rule. You must take heed of his directions. For example, let's say you are earning more money than him, but he can handle your finances better than you can. Are you willing to be the bigger person, swallow your pride, and allow him to assist you? There's nothing wrong with being a boss to your workers, but at home, don't try to boss your man around.

> *"What you want most you push away from you.*
> *You want more than you care to admit."*
>
> —Tarjei Vesaas

You are not considered strong if you are always defensive and if you love challenging your man, and your man should not be considered weak if he chooses not to get involved in your mind games. Keep pushing him away, and he will surely run out the first exit door he sees. Peace of mind is essential to a man's well-being, and compatibility is the ultimate thing that men look for in a relationship. Don't be compelled to drive your man insane—that's ridiculous. Why not concentrate on driving him to achieve success? Ask yourself: If I were a man, could I put up with the things that I do? Would I consider myself weak for avoiding strife?

Strong and confident women aren't as jealous as insecure women, and I admire that. They know that jealousy isn't the same as showing love or respect. They never think that they are too strong to show their man admiration. They reciprocate love. They trust their man's judgments and never question his whereabouts. They know their roles and make their man feel like the king of his castle. That could be you—a strong queen seated beside her king. You can attract the kind of man you deserve by raising or lowering your bar to match his, and by lowering your bar, I do not mean lowering your standards but accepting him for who he is. Be his backbone. Motivate him whenever you see he needs motivation. Inspire him whenever you see he needs inspiration. Guide him back into your arms when he gets lost in the wilderness. We all go through struggles in life. No man is safe from being down and out. But when a man is down and out, it takes a strong woman to help him stand on his feet again. Behind every great man is a great woman. That's the truth.

Being a strong woman doesn't necessarily mean you can't be feminine. Your feminine characteristics are what men are attracted to. You don't have to act macho because being too manly might drive a good man insane. Being strong isn't about being aggressive. It's all about being confident—confidence in yourself and self-assurance that you can be what the Creator created you to be. An independent woman is one who is able to live a good life and also one who is wise enough to realize that having a good man only adds joy to the journey. So the decision is yours: Do you want to live an abundant life with a good man or live a successful and independent life all by yourself? Remember, life is what you make it.

I find successful and independent women very sexy and attractive. They do not intimidate me at all. The way they act toward me determines if I will continue or stop my pursuit. My goal is to connect with who they are as people.

Giving your all, in all areas, will yield the same results. Hold your man accountable for his actions, but keep in mind that everyone makes mistakes and no one is perfect. So don't look down on your man when he does something wrong; help build him up and let your example speak louder than your words.

It amazes me how women can preach how strong and independent they are but expect a man to pay for everything. It's a double standard. We don't expect you to pay, but you should be willing to. It's a small gesture that will go a long way. A relationship is a give-and-take business. You shouldn't need affirmation, chivalry, and guidance, but appreciate them when they are there. Equitable contribution to the relationship is fair. But don't get me wrong; it's not just about money or who pays or plans for stuff. Contributing equally to the relationship doesn't always mean you do everything equally. Your man might pay the bill at the restaurant, and the very next day, you might be making him his favorite home-cooked meal. A system of give and take is the way to go in any relationship.

But someone has to wear the pants and someone has to wear the skirt. A line has to be drawn somewhere, and each person has to know their place within the relationship. As a woman, you must be able to make your man feel like a man. If you want to wear the pants, you are trying to compete with his manhood, and that will always make the situation unattractive. Power and love don't mix, and if you are always competing with your man for position, then your relationship won't last. You and he need to be on the same team and not competing against each other.

I hate when women say, "I have to act tough, like these guys out here, to get what I want." But what exactly does that mean? Women were born strong and have a type of inner strength that men will never have. A man with a dream needs a woman with vision; therefore, you need to recognize that strength within you and use it to build your relationship. Otherwise, your aggressiveness will destroy everything you have worked so hard for. Remember, we all have important differences that allow us to give and to receive, but at the end of the day, we all want to be received. If your strong sense of character is too overbearing and is making your man feel inadequate as a man, it means that you will continue to struggle until you adapt, because no man wants his potential life partner to be that way.

RAE HOLLIDAY

Are you are extremely weak in one particular area, but you are not willing to compromise your ideals because you don't want to give your partner the upper hand? Are you living in denial and don't want to admit that you are weak because you don't want to be vulnerable? If so, I want you to know that you have to be vulnerable or else your relationship won't work. You have to admit your strengths and weaknesses, and then you have to find out your partner's strengths and weaknesses. Only then can you and your man build a lasting relationship and grow as a couple.

The keyword in any relationship is *compromise*. When you're in a loving situation, and a committed one, you and your partner have to be on the same playing field. You can't allow yourself to be too powerful in one area and lackadaisical in others.

You have to be well balanced in all areas. I know we all have our strengths and weaknesses. But compromising should be the way you play off your man's strengths and weaknesses. The relationship shouldn't be all about you. It should be about you and your man getting to know each other. But that's only half the battle. The other half is maintaining the relationship by helping each other grow, because without relationship growth, the love seed that you and your man planted won't see the light of day.

You have to be a blessing in your relationship before your relationship can be a blessing to you. Let me say that again: You have to be a blessing in your relationship before your relationship can be a blessing to you. You have to build your partner up to a point where he's strong in areas where he was once weak. If he has money issues and you're amazing at handling money, then it's your duty to manage his finances and teach him how to handle his money. Give it your all, and all that you get back will astound you.

JICKAEL BAZIN

What is the purpose of a relationship? The best answer I've ever been given comes from one of my mentors on this subject who said to me, "The purpose of a relationship is to magnify the human experience."

There is something inexplicable that happens when this connection occurs between people and they are able to share their emotions and fears. The word *sharing* means giving a portion of something to another; it's the art of giving, not receiving.

Relationships are about sharing, and the quality of your relationship will depend on the amount of time you and your man share with each other. If you're with him just to get what you can out of him, then you are doing a business transaction and not being loyal to the relationship. You both must be willing to give 100 percent to your relationship. But when you start measuring how much you are giving to the relationship, it's over. When it becomes, "I did this, and I did that," when it's managed by rules and not by love, then the relationship is doomed.

Everyone needs rules in order to feel secure. However, the more rules you apply, the more pain you will endure in your relationship. If you can make a conscious decision that your relationship is about magnifying the goodness in your man and that you are going to give unconditionally, then you will receive tenfold in return.

Being strong and decisive are two very attractive qualities. Knowing what you want out of life, having a vision for where you want to be, believing that you too can succeed and make a mark on this male-dominated society—these are all characteristics that are attractive to men who have similar traits, and in order to effectively magnify your experience, as well as his, there must already be common interests, values, and goals that you can both expand on. Remember: eagles do not fly with pigeons!

This does not mean that opposites do not attract, but in the course of doing the research and interviews for this work, the majority of men who are currently in long-term relationships, as well as those who have taken the leap to marriage, were all in agreement that there must be several common core interests and values that a man and woman share in order for their relationship to have a stable foundation to build upon.

Ultimately, it is not about who is stronger or weaker in any capacity. It is about respectfully understanding the other person's strengths and weaknesses, and, from there, determining your individual roles and harnessing your combined strengths while consistently working together toward achieving your short- and long-term relationship goals.

DR. JEAN ALERTE

Some women have accepted the fact that they are the breadwinners in their households. Some women also feel that by being the breadwinner, the relationship is out of balance. This is a social construct that receives too much acceptance from people. Just because society says something is supposed to be a certain way that doesn't mean it's foolproof. You must create your own reality. Go with the flow that doesn't insult your soul. This should not negate the fact that you are partners and can equally provide different levels of support and security. Don't let the material possessions or achievements that you can create and build up together become the things that divide and conquer your relationship. Value the person for the love they have for you. You can't take money with you when you are gone, and it can't buy happiness, health, or love. Focus on creating a world of love around you and the universe gives back extra. It's called good karma.

Do you consider a man unemployed aspiring towards higher education or a man struggling to build his own business weak? Every day, this man defies the odds by maintaining a job or business, and every morning, he wakes up with a burning desire to be better than he was the day before. You must understand that, just because he's not willing to deal with any additional pressures at this time is his life, it does not make him weak. If you label him weak, you are expressing your disapproval of him and what he is trying to do. Support each other's challenges and you will find a friend in him—and possibly a life partner. Everyone has thoughts of living the best life they can possibly live, so never knock a man who has a vision; perhaps he just needs a true ally.

> *"If you can't deal with not being in control, I can assure you that you will struggle with true love."*
> —Stephan Labossiere

I try to avoid drama at all cost, so if there is something undesirable about what my wife is saying, I'll try to diffuse it. That doesn't mean I'm weak or she's too strong; it simply means I choose to remain calm and at peace during our moments of turmoil. I am strong enough to remain calm, to avoid escalating a disagreement. However, too many men debate and argue, knowing that a dispute dampens the mood. The wise know this is not the best way to handle conflict, and they look for logical ways to keep the peace. Women who insult their men by calling them weak should take a step back and examine how they are responding. You can't control another person's behavior, but you can control yours. Do some research if you want to help your man see another viewpoint. Suggest ways in which others have success-fully handled similar issues and allow him to consider it as well as develop his own opinion, and your man will appreciate you more.

It's not in most men's nature to argue. Men are more predisposed to aggression expressed through physical action. I don't reference that to suggest domestic vio-lence, but rather to compare this behavior to a football game. If your man doesn't want to argue with you, this does not mean that he's weak. It possibly alludes to the exact opposite, that he possesses an inner strength to make the intelligent decision to exit the situation. It's a wiser choice because nothing can be solved with vio-lence. Violence begets violence.

Matthew 7:1 states, "Do not judge or you too will be judged." Your man is human, just like you, and makes mistakes, just like you. So try to understand the situation he is in, instead of reacting to it emotionally. If your man can't find compassion and understanding in you, he will feel separate from you and perhaps alone. Your man needs a partner who can impart wisdom and knowledge that can aid his quest. He will not accept answers that do not make sense to his soul and are based on conditions within his environment. Someone said, "A person con-vinced against his will is of the same opinion still, and if you plan on telling him the truth, then be prepared to face the anger and resentment to follow." Too much power is given to the thought of rejection, and rejection should not get any power. We should never let our fears determine our choices. Fears will only block your journey and keep you stagnant. Understand the unfriendly environment in which fear lives. You can either continue to fear everything and run, or you can face everything and rise together. A great assessment of the situation will balance your judgment. Also, recognize the resiliency of your nature, and seek to resolve the problems within you first. Learn how to build your foundation through love for yourself and others. When your foundation is firmly rooted in good soil, growth is possible, and what you and your man have will stand the test of time.

Kel Spencer

"Question. Tell me what you think about me? I buy my own diamonds and I buy my own rings. Only ring your celly when I'm feelin' lonely. When it's all over, please get up and leave. Question."

—Destiny's Child

There is something that the United States of America, Roc Nation (formerly Roc-A-Fella Records), and Rochelle Stein have in common. What they share is a desire to no longer be a part of the system that they once were attached to. What they share is disgust towards what once was, with an attraction towards doing things in a new way on their own terms. They all have made a Declaration of Independence, and I believe that independence is a wonderful thing when progression is its offspring.

In my dorm room at Morgan State University, I remember picking up the phone to call my dad. It was spring semester of my sophomore year. I was nervous because my roommate and I had just borrowed a car to go and look at apartments. We found a few that we liked, and we began putting our sales pitch together on how to approach our parents about moving off campus. We already had plans to work that summer, to save money for our first cars. Can you imagine how we would look, being superstars on campus with cars but still living on campus as juniors? Like, really, who does that? So we put our pitches together and then flipped a coin to see who would call first.

I lost the coin toss and reluctantly dialed my parents' number. My father picked up, and he was in a great mood. The pressure increased because I didn't want my pitch to disrupt his joy, but I jumped right in and asked, "Dad, can I move off campus next year?"

He replied, "You want to move off campus? Why?" I gave a whole song and dance about the apartment being close to the campus, and how I could focus better in the seclusion of my own home, and how being independent would teach me a great deal of responsibility. But deep down, my main goal was to increase my social status and have a place of my own—somewhere where I could exchange bodily fluids with Jasmine, Shannon, Allison, Michelle, Kemelyne (when they came down from New York to visit me), and Vanessa and a few others. But I had to give my dad the appetizer while withholding the main meal. Anyway, I stated my case, and then there was complete silence. I became worried, and after a few seconds, my dad finally replied, "I think it's an excellent idea." I was excited. His reason was that having my own apartment would teach me independence, and shortly afterward, I signed my first leased agreement and felt like Benjamin Franklin and his fifty-five colleagues, or Sean Carter at Roc Nation with his attorneys. Finally, just like them, I had declared my independence, and I disassociated myself from my former dormitory way of life.

The problem with independence is this—there's a huge difference between wanting no part of a system and knowing how to do for yourself while participating in that system. One is called being independent and the other is called being self-sufficient.

An independent woman will more than likely stay independent, and a good man will always love her independence. One of my favorite quotes is found in the movie *300*, when Leonidas was about to go to war with the Persians. His wife, Queen Gorgo, in a calm and still voice said, "It is not a question of what a Spartan citizen should do, nor a husband nor a king. Instead, ask yourself, my dearest love, what should a free man do?" Those were powerful words of wisdom, and Queen Gorgo's question was meant to ignite action. She didn't tell her husband whatever he wanted to hear. She didn't give him some lame answer like, "Baby, whatever you want to do." No, she gave him the hard and honest truth. And shortly afterward, in that scene, he gave her the same.

So, ladies, your man wants you to be strong—the same strength that you would want to see in him. But know that strength is never about how loud or how visually convincing you can be. True strength possesses the ability to be gentle. True strength houses control. True strength contains a meek button. Be strong, and don't ever tell your man, "I don't need a man for anything!" Because doing so would be similar to shooting yourself in the foot. Your man already knows that you don't need a man. Just like peanut butter doesn't need jelly, but they make a powerful combination. So why not be together? A man needs to be needed. He doesn't need a ruler or a tyrant, but he does need to feel like he's an important part of the equation. Question.

Life Coach Note
by Pervis Taylor

I can't tell you how many times I've heard my female clients ask "Why are men afraid of a strong woman?"

My answer is always the same: "What is a strong woman?" Through my own personal journey, I've come to know that strength is a more inward expression than outward appearance. Some of the most emotionally unstable people appear to be strong because they look like what perceived strength is: bold, no nonsense, "I speak my mind" type of thing. That's not being strong. Strength is more spiritual. Strength means to endure hardship and still be supportive of others. Strength is knowing that you've been hurt but being brave enough to try to love again. Strength is having the weight of the world on your shoulders and having the audacity to dream for a better life. Ladies, if this is you, then by all means, you are indeed a strong woman. However, if you are the "I don't take no mess" attitude under the guise of being a strong woman, you, sadly, more often than not, will find yourself continuing to ask that question.

Being strong is also being vulnerable and allowing your heart to be received or rejected by another. I'm not going to lie; there are some men who are intimidated by a truly strong woman. But guess what? You don't need them! There is a man out there who is strong enough to handle your heart. You just focus on being a good thing and let him find you. Additionally, remember you are strong when you can admit that you need help or that you don't have all the answers. Believe it or not, men find it attractive when a woman doesn't act like she has it all together.

4

CAN YOU HANDLE
THE TRUTH?

FRANK GATEAU

We all have heard of love at first sight. Perhaps we don't know how real that concept is, but I definitely believe in lust at first sight. The main objective of lust at first sight is to have sex with the object of your lust, and if there happens to be an emotional connection, that's an extra bonus. "Hi, can I get to know you?" sounds way more appealing than, "Hi, I can't wait to have sex with you." There's a big difference between liking, lusting, and loving. A man has to be aware of his actions and realize what emotion he is experiencing.

A lot of times, women ask questions like, "Do I look fat in this?" If you're asking me this, then the answer is probably, "Yes!" But that is not what women want to hear when the "Am I fat?" question is being asked. And when a man tells them the truth, they will say he is being insensitive, while in reality, he is just telling it like it is. So ask yourself this question: Do you want your man to be sensitive to your feelings or tell you the truth?

Let's face it—the truth hurts, and many times women ask questions that they really don't want to know the answers to because knowing the truth doesn't aid them in understanding the issue, and most certainly it doesn't take away the pain. So, for better or worse, lies are a part of your relationship, and whether you look at that from a moral or ethnical standpoint, the reality is always there, and sometimes we are forced to lie when dealing with certain situations. Oftentimes, men lie to protect the other person. But a man's intention is never to hurt his woman but to keep the peace.

Men look at stuff rationally and weigh the pros and cons, and it's easy for women to not understand that men tell lies as a necessity, in an attempt to stay in their women's good grace.

A woman once told me, "I can only offer you great sex and, depending on the day, a good conversation. But anything else, you have the wrong woman." She was brutally honest about her intentions. She wasn't looking for love, marriage, or a relationship. She just wanted sex! I appreciated her for being so honest and direct. I knew what to expect, and what not to expect, from her. The relationship was transparent, even though I believed it wasn't possible for a woman to be in a sexual relationship without some type of emotional attachment forming. But imagine if that situation were the other way around, and I had told her or another woman that all I had to offer to her was sex. Do you think she would've accepted my offer? Maybe but probably not, but this particular woman knew I could handle the truth. I didn't look down on her or place judgment, because we were both in agreement.

It's risky for men to be straightforward with women because the truth doesn't always yield the results we are intending, and when we are being direct with our women, our messages can sometimes go in one ear and out the other. So lies are perpetuated to get our women to listen to us. Even though a lie is a lie, there are also levels of lying. Secrets should not be kept, and whenever your man lies, it's probably because he wants to protect your feelings. Can you handle that truth? Don't get me wrong; there are guys out there that selfishly lie for their own personal gain, and most of them lie about having a girlfriend, a wife, children, second or third families, etc. But those lies are the ones where any excuse doesn't have any merit. I'm not sticking up for those types of guys, only for the ones that are sincere. So, yes! There are sincere lies, and there's a difference between lying and hiding things.

*"A little sincerity is a dangerous thing, and a great deal
of it is absolutely fatal."*
—Oscar Wilde

Oftentimes, the problem is in how we communicate.
Knowing that you can't handle the truth puts your man
in an awkward situation. He has to be careful about how
he answers you because the truth might trigger an argument. So, for the sake of peace, he might tell you, "You
look great!" even though you might look slightly better
than decent. Or he might say, "I love your cooking!"
even though it might taste like jail food. These spur-of-
the-moment lies cause the problem to continue and the
relationship suffers because you can't handle the truth.
Rather then being labeled as insensitive or heartless,
your man might see lying as a way to avoid conflict.

But women don't like when men lie, and they hate
when men tell them the awful truth. To them, lying is a
turn-off and the truth is a death sentence. If you are this
type of woman, ask yourself: Why does my man withhold the truth from me? It's probably because most of
the time, the truth will not get him what he wants. Yes,
"the truth shall set you free," but in the dating and relationship game, the truth can cause you more harm than
good. The truth isn't always rewarding, and you will oftentimes get punished for telling it. But remember—your

man wants to be heard and understood just as much as you do, and he might not like admitting to failures in his life, career, and relationships. But bear with him. You see, with lies, you have to handle things carefully, whether they are small or big.

> *"Fiction was invented the day Jonah arrived home and told his wife that he was three days late because he had been swallowed by a whale."*
> —Gabriel García Márquez

I can't speak for other men, but I hate being accused of something I didn't do. Wouldn't you? So don't punish or accuse your man of something he didn't do, because eventually that will make him want to do it. If you and the guy you are dating are not in a committed relationship, can you handle him telling you that you are one of many women that he is seeing? Probably not, because no woman wants to hear that she is a second or third string, so the best thing you can do is establish what you are looking for and see if your man fits in your equation, without putting any added pressure on him. Watch his actions, because they will speak louder than his words.

Every relationship boils down to trust, but trust must be earned. A lot of times, women blame men for thinking like men.

When the truth is handled correctly, you will grow as a person and your relationship will reach new heights. Basically, when you stop punishing men for speaking truthfully, the less you will have to worry about lies.

RAE HOLLIDAY

"Integrity is telling myself the truth. And honesty is telling the truth to other people."
—Spencer Johnson

Can you handle the truth? When love shows up at your door, will you accept all that comes along with it? In life, there's good truth, and there's bad truth. Are you ready to feel the pain that hearing a truth can cause? Love is not always kind. It can be amazing, but it's not always kind. Sometimes a lie, coming out of a compassionate heart, can really do some good in an unjust world. Many times, what you think is going on in your relationship is really not; sometimes it's just a smoke screen. Sometimes you may think the man that you're with is treating you with the utmost respect, treating you in a way that's just wonderful and amazing, until you step outside the box and have conversations with other women who are in relationships. Then, you start to realize your relationship, which you thought was peaches and cream is not so great. I know the truth hurts. But by now, you should be immune to its pain.

> *"You can't put a price tag on love. But if you could,*
> *I'd wait for it to go on sale."*
> —Jarod Kintz

Years of being in a committed relationship with you might cause your man to become sluggish. His sluggishness might cause him to misuse future earnings. He wants to tell you what's wrong, but he's afraid of letting you down. So he tells you a lie, thinking it's the solution to his problems. But when you find out the truth, how will you react? How would you feel if you found out that his mother knows more about your relationship than you do? You see, love comes with a price tag. Many times, it's an emotional, psychological, or physical price. It can come in so many different forms, but one thing is for certain: love always comes with a price. It's never free.

JICKAEL BAZIN

> *"The truth is incontrovertible. Malice may attack it,*
> *ignorance may deride it, but in the end there it is."*
> —Winston Churchill

A large percentage of relationships meet their doom simply because someone lied about something, and if a relationship is built on a lie, then surely it will meet its doom. No matter how deeply a lie may be buried, in due time, it will find its way to the surface.

But what is considered a lie? In my opinion, it's the act of altering the truth to avoid pain. This pain may be described as embarrassment, fear of loss, a bad reflection of character, or anything that you feel, in the moment, will cause you to feel inadequate or inferior. It's a natural human instinct to avoid pain, especially when the result of that pain is in direct conflict to your human needs. Based on this, do we intentionally lie as a natural reaction to avoid pain? Wouldn't it be much simpler to tell the truth now and avoid the pain later?

But let's not get too ahead of ourselves, because there are many ways to interpret a lie given its context. If you are dating a man and he portrays himself as a certain type of individual, but after a few weeks together, you find out that, although he may be a good man, some things he led you to believe were not necessarily true, then he may have embellished a bit or omitted something from his past for you. At that point, you would probably wonder what you should do. In my opinion, I believe there are three ways to address this situation.

1. How do you grade the lie, and on what level will this newfound truth affect your relationship?
2. Can you work through this obstacle with communication?
3. Now that the damage has been done, can you reaffirm the trust in your relationship?

A lie is a lie, no matter how you cut it. It's the act of intentionally altering what happened or was said, heard, or seen. In a relationship, there are lies we can and cannot live with. There are those we choose to forgive and work through, and then there are lies that cut us to a point of no return. We tend to grade the lie based on the level of pain it causes us and how it will affect the trust we have in the other person. The grade of lie determines the steps that need to be taken in order to find a solution. A lie may or may not cause you enough pain to end your relationship, and if you choose to work things out, then you can use communication to try and solve your problem. I believe that communication is the number-one factor in having a healthy relationship. Your ability to effectively communicate your thoughts, feelings, fears, and anger will determine if your relationship will survive or fall victim to dishonesty, which is the major pothole in relationships today.

"The naked truth is always better than the best-dressed lie."
—Ann Landers

It's very important that you express the pain that a lie has caused. Explain to your man why you have decided to work through the lie. Clarify why it is important for him to be truthful at all times and that you will be expecting nothing but the truth from him. Demanding honesty should be viewed as establishing an unwritten clause between you and your man, and you should also understand that this is not the time to take advantage of his guilt or to make him beg at your feet. Remember, commitment is doing something you said you were going to do long after the feeling you had when you said it has passed. I am a firm believer that you will be able to handle the truth. The challenge comes in how you will respond based on the level of pain it causes you.

DR. JEAN ALERTE

"In the heart of the nation's capital, in a courthouse of the US government, one man will stop at nothing to keep his honor, and one will stop at nothing to find the truth."
—*A Few Good Men's* tagline

In the blockbuster film *A Few Good Men*, navy lawyer Lieutenant Daniel Kaffee (played by Tom Cruise) exposes Colonel Nathan R. Jessup (played by Jack Nicholson). Kaffee brings to light Jessup's false testimony surrounding the death of a Marine named Santiago, and when pressed hard by Kaffee to tell the truth, Colonel Jessup snappishly yells, "You can't handle the truth! Son, we live in a world that has walls, and those walls have to be guarded by men with guns. Who's gonna do it? You? You, Lieutenant Weinberg? I have a greater responsibility than you can possibly fathom. You weep for Santiago and you curse the marines. You have that luxury. You have the luxury of not knowing what I know: that Santiago's death, while tragic, probably saved lives. And my existence, while grotesque and incomprehensible to you, saves lives. You don't want the truth because deep down, in places you don't talk about at parties, you want me on that wall! You need me on that wall! We use words like *honor, code, loyalty.* We use these words as the backbone of a life spent defending something. You use them as a punch line. I have neither the time nor the inclination to explain myself to a man who rises and sleeps under the blanket of the very freedom that I provide, and then questions the manner in which I provide it! I would rather you just said thank you and went on your way. Otherwise, I suggest you pick up a weapon and stand a post. Either way, I don't give a damn what you think you are entitled to!"

Kaffee walks up to Jessup and asks, "Did you order the code red?"

Jessup begins, "I did the job you—"

Kaffee yells at Jessup, "Did you order the code red?"

And then finally, Jessup fires back, "You're goddamn right I did!"

I don't know about you, but I see a direct correlation between Kaffee and Jessup's heated courtroom dialogue and the arguments that many couples have when one person in the relationship wants answers, but the other person is trying to hide the truth.

Sometimes, your man might lie to protect your feelings, because he might feel that you can't handle the truth. And if you keep pressing him, you might hear something you don't want to hear. So use wisdom to decipher whether your man is telling you the truth or not. The later part of Matthew 10:16 states, "Be wise as serpents and harmless as doves." Listen carefully to the words coming out of your man's mouth, and read between the lines, but don't assume. Give him that amount of respect. You see the truth is light, and the only way for us to evolve as human beings is to live in the light. Lying is a terrible habit that should be rectified immediately; however, some people avoid living in the light because they don't want anyone to view them as being ugly or unpleasant, and I believe when a woman shows that she can handle the truth, the whole truth, and nothing but the truth, then her man feels comfortable telling her the truth. But if she can't handle the truth, then an argument might arise out of nowhere when she is told the truth.

Conflicts form personality traits, which turn into the complexities of one's character. Wisdom is required in order to recognize something is off in the relationship in the beginning. You should not overlook or make excuses for behaviors that insult the integrity of the relationship or undermine your intelligence. Hear the words as truthful when your man speaks to you. Don't assume or read between the lines. Both people should be held accountable solely because of the energy they wield over another. The majority of the time, one is more expressive than another or, as some would say, one loves the other more. However, if the relationship is not healthy, you will feel it in your heart. The heart doesn't lie. The relationship needs to be reevaluated and a decision needs to be made. The objective is to determine if your man is equally invested in the relationship and in it for the long haul or if your man is just passing time until someone more suitable is found. The question you must ask yourself is: How much does he care for my well-being? The answer should be enough for you to not make excuses for any bad behavior. Self-love is a true test of your spirit, which will not allow you to stay in a relationship that harms your soul. However, some people can't handle the truth, and it causes friction and ends in an argument or fight. The choice between being brutally honest with yourself or lying to avoid friction will reveal how much self-love you have. You must care for your emotional well-being before you expect for someone else too.

Kel Spencer

"The truth will set you free, but first it will piss you off."
—Gloria Steinem

It was spring of 2003, and my girl and I had been together for three years. This was my first real relationship, and I thought she would be the one I'd marry. But before going that extra mile, I wanted to line things up a bit. What I mean is this—for the first year of our relationship, I cheated like a mad man. And I don't mean, one here and another there. I'm talking about the type of state-to-state, country-to-country, passport stamp, two keys to women's apartments, disgusting, male-whore type cheating. At the end of year one, I came to a breaking point—I wanted to grow up.

So I straightened up my act, and for some strange reason, I felt she should know what I had done in the past. Some may say I was simply being honest—or too honest perhaps. Some people (like my sister Christina) called my honesty plain old stupidity. But I believed my girl deserved the truth—even though she didn't ask to hear it. I believed she was entitled to know everything about me, and I wanted to be transparent. So, prior to having this sit-down with her, I consulted Christina, and she told me I needed to let it go because it was all in the past. But again, I had my reasons for wanting to be truthful with my girlfriend. "Don't no chick wanna hear that!" Christina said. "She ain't gon' know what to do with that information. It's best you keep that info to yourself because it ain't current." I took in what she said and came up with a new plan.

About a week went by, and I told my girlfriend that I wanted to talk. I made sure that this talk was conveniently the night before I left for L.A. That way, we would either fight and have space, or the dialogue would go extremely well. I sat her down and told her that there were some things that I had lied about. My logic for this approach was—if she wanted to know the details, then she would ask, but if she didn't want to know the details, then she wouldn't ask. But either way, at least I was putting my honest foot forward. Not only did she ask, but she also asked about specific studio sessions, specific flights to specific cities, and specific times when I was on the phone talking low. She asked about specific women she had suspicions of. Some of it I was guilty of and some of it I wasn't. Suffice it to say, that conversation was the beginning of our end. We lasted about five months after that, off and on and then finally, on my birthday, November 8, 2003, I cut it off; that conversation had been the reason why she had then cheated on me two months later, weeks after saying she appreciated my honesty. She said, "Most men wouldn't tell the truth about that stuff, but you did, and I appreciate it. I forgive you." And after cheating on me, she said, "So what? You did it too."

The truth was told, but did I have to tell it? I'm still not sure. Is the truth the reason why we broke up? Not sure about that either. But what I do know is this—life happened, and for better or worse, it wasn't until the truth was told that things went sour. I really don't think any of us want to know the 100 percent truth about our significant others. Do you really want to know which coworker your man has a meaningless crush on? Do you want to know that he hates how you look in your favorite dress? Or do you want to know that the bathroom door was slightly opened and he accidentally saw your sister naked—and kept looking? Do you really want to know that? I doubt it. The truth should absolutely receive the praises and high regard that it gets because it is the principle of the thing. The truth is absolutely the fulcrum for justice and balance, but some truths need to be hidden—not necessarily out of malice or dishonesty, but sometimes for our protection.

LIFE COACH NOTE
by Pervis Taylor

Truth is always confrontational. The reality is, most of us live our version of the truth. Moreover, we've become comfortable living in delusion. How many times have women felt in their hearts and spirits that their men were cheating and said nothing? How many times have we known something was wrong and acted like it wasn't? The truth is scary and brings everything front and center. We all say we want an honest mate, but when it boils down to it, do we truly want that? As a life coach, one of my greatest challenges is exposing my clients to the truth. They often get upset with me, but in the end, they come back grateful and, most importantly, changed. The truth is the only foundation for a relationship that will truly stand the test of time. You can have devotion, loyalty, love, kindness, but if there's deception involved, eventually that union will dissolve. We, as humans, don't like to admit that we are judgmental. We all have pasts; some sordid and some down-right crazy. But if we say we want honesty, we have to be mature enough to handle each other's reality. Are you mature enough to be with a man who was molested as a child? Are you mature enough to be with a man who has gone to prison? Are you mature enough to be with a man who has been with hundreds of women and had STDs? These questions only begin to scratch the surface. Truth is indeed stranger than fiction. One of the best ways to remedy this is for you to get raw and truthful with yourself. Once you can embrace the rawness of your life, you, in turn, will be able to embrace the rawness of another's life.

5

THE GOOD, THE BAD, AND THE UGLY

FRANK GATEAU

Women want men to give them the world, and there are certainly good men out there who are capable of doing that, but unfortunately, these men go unnoticed because women are constantly looking for Mr. Right in all the wrong places. Even though there is technically no wrong place, there are places that can yield the certain type of guy you are looking for better than others. For instance, you can't expect to find a man who is a homebody when 90 percent of the men you meet are in nightclubs and bars. You will probably hear women saying, "There are no good men out there," not knowing that there is a good supply of good men in many places that they have yet to go to. No one can predict where he or she will find love, but picking the right setting is very important in finding a good man.

Women should know what they want, but I feel that when they see it, or when they have it in their possession, they either overlook it or are dissatisfied with it. You hear it all the time, "Why do good girls like bad guys?" That's because these types of women seek excitement; they want adventure. I'm not saying that good men can't provide those things, but the jerks and so-called "bad guys" are usually great at keeping a woman up on her toes. There's a reason why people say, "Nice guys finish last." It's because, unfortunately, they do.

> *"Men will treat you the way you let them. There is no such thing as 'deserving' respect; you get what you demand from people...if you demand respect, he will either respect you or he won't associate with you."*
> —Tucker Max

You should reevaluate what's more important to you: the short- or long-term relationship? Analyze the pros and cons. If the pros outweigh the cons, then go for it, but if it's the other way around, then you should run for help. Ask yourself this question: Am I simply buying what he is selling, or do I really like him? No one is perfect, and everyone comes with some type of emotional or physical baggage.

It's easier for a man to find a suitable woman than for a woman to find a fitting man. Some women think they can change and mold men into what they want them to be. If a man changes because of a woman, it's only because he wanted to change. You cannot force it. Also, as long as you allow a man to test-drive your product, without having to buy it, that's exactly what he will continue to do.

All love is not real love. Some love is lustful. Oftentimes, women date men who have no intentions of marrying them. These men want sex, and the last thing on their minds is commitment. So after being constantly heartbroken by these types of men, some women become bitter and start to show men-like tendencies. From experience, they learn to withhold their true emotions and start dating multiple men, and in the process, they become aggressive, irrational, and distrusting. So, take a step back, look in the mirror and ask yourself: Would I bring me home to meet my parents?

A woman should be morally admired, but nowadays, a virtuous woman is hard to find. Whatever happened to the women who displayed classy characteristics, who were caring, supportive, trustworthy, faithful, and loyal? We need them back. Two wrongs don't make a right, so don't let your past prohibit you from finding the man that is right for you. Of course, men are partially to blame for the many misguided women out there. A healthy relationship is one that consists of two people motivating each other, bringing the best out of one another. Anything other than that is a waste of time. You cannot find the right person until you become right with yourself. Look at the relationship between your man and his mother. Is it healthy? And if so, can you incorporate some of his mother's good characteristics?

I heard a story of a woman who cheated on her man for an entire summer with a fling she had no real intention of being in a committed relationship with. Maybe she wanted to make him jealous or wanted to feel wanted, or maybe she was just very promiscuous. Who knows? She ending up getting pregnant by her boyfriend, and nine months later, she gave birth to a beautiful set of twin girls. She hoped that the children would somehow bring her and her boyfriend closer together. But all her wishful thinking was in vain. She and her boyfriend broke up before the babies could even take their first steps. Hurt beyond belief, the woman clung to her summer fling, and they became closer. She now wanted to explore the option of them being an item, but the fling never took her seriously. He knew her ways and didn't want to be one of her victims. He resented the fact that she already had two babies with another man, a man whom she had cheated on with him. He believed in karma and knew that, whoever he was in a committed relationship with, he would not want to be on the other end of that treachery. What goes around comes around, right? How could he possibly instill his trust in someone as disloyal and dishonest as she was? She didn't even feel any remorse for stepping out on her man, so when everything came tumbling down, she fell hard and learned a valuable lesson: there is either a good, bad, or ugly result associated with every decision that we make. Do unto others, as you would like them do unto you. Maybe she liked the feeling of being desired and wanted by other men and that became addictive and overwhelming. But was it worth it? Her image was tainted. Whenever she looked in the mirror, she saw an unwanted person. We all are tested at one point or another, but only those with strong willpower will pass the true test.

Men will date women whom they like but have no intentions of marrying. Men are sex-orientated creatures, and emotions and commitment comes after.

The most common form of communication, when making a first impression, is nonverbal. Body language and self-presentation are extremely important. We dislike women who are habitual flirters. Too much flirting will make you look promiscuous. Another turn-off is a woman who parties all the time. How can I take you seriously? Unless you're getting paid to be at parties, you shouldn't be in a nightclub every other day. Bringing up marriage too soon is also another no-no. Avoid it at all cost. If anything, let your man bring it up. But definitely don't bring it up if you and your man have only been together for a short period of time.

Social media provides us with more ways than ever to connect one person to another, but unfortunately, it has separated people just as much. The Internet makes confronting someone a lot easier now, and many relationships are suffering. Consider the saying "the grass is greener on the other side." Well, now you can actually see just how green it is through Facebook, Twitter, Instagram, and other popular dating apps and websites. Everything is revealed in real time for the world to see. It's a gift and a curse, and you should use good judgment when posting information, especially if you are in a relationship. All these new social media platforms have allowed men to ask for exactly what they want and expect—instant gratification. There's less value placed on sex because it is easily available in a wide variety of options. And with the amount of competition, it's harder to capture and sustain a man's attention. All of that is damaging our generation's ability to maintain relationships. That is what you are fighting against. But the trick is being able to identify the good, the bad, and the ugly. You have to demand respect and also give it back. Good men do exist, but you have to be able to identify them.

"No matter how plain a woman may be, if truth and honesty are written across her face, she will be beautiful."
—Eleanor Roosevelt

At first, most of your relationships will be used as learning experiences. It's a new day and age when it comes to dating. It has always been a competitive sport. If you don't see it as such, then you need to take another look and adapt to the new landscape of dating. Using the old ways and methods will not give you new results. Some women are being more aggressive in their tactics while still remaining ladies and keeping it tasteful. Don't be afraid to be the first to start a conversation. Buy the man you want a drink. That's definitely a way to get his attention. Women who are hip to the game are winning. A woman can't just show up and expect her appearance to be the gift. She just can't go out with a guy, eat all the food on her plate or enjoy the Broadway play, and not expect to reciprocate the generosity. Life doesn't work that way. So make yourself approachable. Looking stuck-up ruins your chances of getting picked up. If something isn't working, change your game plan and try something else. Be spontaneous and you will win. Sex will not keep a guy, your personality will, your character will, and your attitude will.

Another truth of the matter is that a lot of relation-ships you encounter and build with men are just prepara-tion for that guy to be a better man for the woman after you. It's like you're grooming and guiding the perfect guy for another woman. I've learned and grown after every relationship I've had with women, whether casual or committed. You just have to hope that the man you want has completed that process when you get to him.

"Time is what we want most but what we use worst."
—William Penn

You can always gain money back but not time. This is why I walk away from a bad situation as soon as I real-ize it's not what I want or I notice there are too many games being played, and you should too. Start paying close attention to the amount of time you are spend-ing with someone. Is it a waste of time, or is there real potential for growth? Where time is being spent is a true indicator of what type of relationship you are in. A healthy relationship takes time, effort, and commit-ment. So don't focus on things that are detrimental to your relationship, build instead of destroying. Make time for what you really want. No matter how busy your schedule might be, find time. A balanced life is key to maintaining a healthy relationship. People make time for whatever it is that they want, no matter how busy the schedule or heavy the workload. Don't put 100 percent of your best years into not exploring life.

RAE HOLLIDAY

When I was younger and a tad bit inexperienced, I would give the advice to my friends when they came to me with their relationship dramas. I felt like I had a good head on my shoulders, even though I wasn't in a relationship. I was always keen on treating people the way I wanted to be treated. As I reminisce about those therapeutic sessions, I can recall giving a few awful pieces of advice to my friends. When they were cheated on or lied to, my advice would always be to bail—don't stick around, don't deal with it, that's not what you're here for, and that's not real love! I was always quick to tell them to break it off instead of working it out.

But the key is to enter a relationship knowing that there will be good, bad, and ugly times. There are many levels to commitment, and every year, the level of your commitment to your man will have to increase in order for you and him to experience real growth.

As an adult, after seeing the error of my ways and after having been through a few relationships, I can now see that every relationship comes with the good, the bad, and the ugly. There's no perfect relationship. It's really about what you want as far as love and commitment is concerned. Once you get to the point where love starts to seep into your heart, and you can't live without your man, that means it's time to get ready for the good, the bad, and the ugly. You can't run away from it; it's coming because it's inevitable.

Jickael Bazin

Every so often, I hear women saying, "Good men are hard to find," and a slight chuckle escapes me every time. My reply is always, "What's your definition of a good man?" Some women have no idea what they want in a man, and others has an ideal vision of the man they want, but then the question becomes: Is that portrait concurrent with the vision and goals that she has set for herself?

The law of attraction is so powerful that you will attract whatever you put out there in the universe. Your predominant thought is what you will gravitate toward. Therefore, whomever you are thinking about or the image of the man you hold dearly in your mind will gravitate toward you. But is that vision aligned with the vision and standards that you hold for yourself? You must make sure the thoughts that you put out there are pure and exactly the way you want them to be. Otherwise, you could be setting yourself up for unhappy times.

In today's world, with the news, social, and flash media, most men want to be seen, heard, and recognized. Other men chose to live vicariously through someone else's hype, and they use this hype as a spider uses its web—to catch something. Deception leaves a foggy haze, and usually clouds a woman's vision of what's real and what's not. The guy who genuinely believes in traditional courting—meaning the guy who is able to provide the love and trust in a relationship—usually ends up hearing, "You drive a what? You make how much money? How are we supposed to live on that?" It's sad, but these types of women will stay single or accept guys that will risk everything and worry about the consequences later.

> *"Money cannot buy peace of mind. It cannot heal ruptured relationships, or build meaning into a life that has none."*
> —Richard M. DeVos

A woman needs to make the decision early on in life that she does not need a man for financial growth but rather as a companion, a partner who will help her discover new things and experience the vast pleasures of life.

Through the process of writing this book, I've heard countless stories from single ladies who have, in their past, met men they considered to be good, men who have had all the characteristics and values that were attractive enough for these women to take notice, but the common denominator of money was always the deal breaker, whether it was how much he earned or how much he was willing to spend. These stories, all very similar, also have the same outcome: these ladies are still looking for the right guy. Although money may be one of the biggest causes of stress, it is only one of the hurdles you will have to get over in building a successful relationship.

It is absolutely ludicrous to think that being in a relationship will be all singing birds, blooming flowers, and sunny skies. In my opinion, the thought of a perfect world, where everything happens exactly as we want it to, is absolutely boring. One of the joys of life is the excitement and anticipation of not knowing what is coming next. All of us, men and women alike, have or should have a plan for our lives, a plan for where we want to be and who we want to become. But we must always be ready to improvise and adjust when things don't go as planned. The same principle applies to your relationships.

Since all human beings have flaws, let's get what should be the obvious out of the way—there is no such thing as "the perfect man," and just like you, any man you date will have his good and bad days. These bad days may vary in cause, but the point is they will happen, and your reaction to his mood swings on these days will have a direct association to whether he keeps the reasons to himself or decides to share his dilemmas with you. Contrary to popular belief, we do have feelings and do sometimes go through our own emotional roller coasters. The last thing a man wants to do after battling the world outside all day is to come home for round two with his lady. The last thing you want to do is turn a bad day into an ugly one. He will look to you for support and sympathy on these days. Although he may not want to discuss the issue at first, you will comfort him and put his mind at ease enough to where he will begin to communicate with you about his sour mood. Your expectations should be that he reciprocate this when you have your bad days.

Surely there will be those times when the bad days you both have are due to a disagreement between the two of you. I cannot stress enough the importance of communication. Even in a heated battle with your man, your ability to effectively share your feelings without getting nasty and saying things purely out of anger can make or break your relationship. You never want to get to the point where things get ugly and you begin to verbally or physically abuse each other. I suggest a cool-down period for both of you before you continue your discussion. This break, however, must be communicated and agreed on by you both. One of you must be levelheaded enough to calmly say to the other, "Babe, we are both heated, and rather than yell at each other and say things we do not mean, let's take a break, calm down, and we can both approach the situation from a calm, thought-out perspective." This may sound unrealistic, but remember, you are both adults and should act accordingly. Sometimes, in order to correct or resolve a situation, you must apply an approach that takes you out of your comfort zone.

DR. JEAN ALERTE

The good—a woman says she wants a good man, a "Cinderella story," and meets one. The bad—when the woman meets the good man, she focuses on frivolous things about him that she feels are unacceptable.

Perhaps he is not stylish, he's boring, he is not the most handsome, or does not have a car. The ugly—she settles down with the guy who has all the characteristics she wants, but the man that she falls in love with does not want to commit to her and does not treat her well.

You should not date or marry a man for his money, degrees, cars, good looks, accolades, or number of followers on social media. You should date or get married to the man's character and not his outer layer.

The good is also being able to work out problems with your man through thick and thin, the bad is the drama caused by not being able to work out problems with your man, and the ugly is when all hell breaks loose in the aftermath. Expect to experience these three conditions when you are in a committed relationship—know that, when you are unhappy, it's only for a season, and remember, you are the master of your relationship, so whichever way you go, expect a new situation to arise, and count it as a blessing that you are able to experience the good, the bad, and the ugly. During these happy and unhappy times, you will gain knowledge, wisdom, and understanding. You will grow as an individual and encounter emotions that you never knew existed, and most importantly, you may experience a dream or nightmare, but remember, there is a blessing in the lesson.

"Dear brothers and sisters, when troubles come your way, consider it an opportunity for great joy."
—James 1:2 (New Living Translation)

How can you appreciate happiness if you haven't experienced unhappiness? And if you are having problems with your man, know that great joy is on its way to comfort the both of you. But you have to remain patient. Absorb the moment and grow in wisdom. Life is a game and love is the prize. Is being loved the most meaningful thing in your life? If so, then nothing should come between you and your destiny with your man. Challenges will arise in your life. Things will be good in the beginning and can turn bad in the middle, but it's up to you not to finish on an ugly note. Allow love to minister to you during your turbulent times and be aware of how you respond to life's events that are detrimental to your well-being, and through it all, you should always strive to have peace of mind.

KEL SPENCER

"When you have to shoot...shoot, don't talk."
—Tuco, *The Good, the Bad, and the Ugly*

There's a difference between stealing and robbing. I can respect a stick-up kid who robs more than I can a thief who steals. It was the summer of 1997, and I was home from school and got robbed. I had on my brand-new Cuban link chain with a diamond-cut scorpion pendant. I had the matching bracelet as well. We were all at a barbecue in Brooklyn, and we were enjoying ourselves. We got a few phone numbers, ate some food, and went on our merry way. As we were walking, a young man walked past me. His vibe felt wrong, so I walked into the street—alongside the cars. Shortly afterward, he walked over to me, holding a revolver, and pointed the instrument of death at my stomach. "You know what this is," he said. I put my hands up, and he took my jewelry and wallet. And as he walked away, he screamed, "Just so you know, it's real!" He aimed his gun and fired two shots in the air. I was a teenager and when I got home, my father could tell something was wrong. I told him what had happened. I was frustrated, embarrassed, and ashamed, so I went to sleep.

I woke up hours later and didn't hear the TV in the living room. Normally, my father would be up at that time, watching the sports highlights. I went into the living room, and the lights were on but the TV was off. I looked outside and all was normal. My father's car was in the driveway. I opened up the front door of our home, and the light inside of my father's car came on, and he screamed, "Yo!" as if he was startled. My father was lying back in the driver's seat, with his head propped up on his bedroom pillow, with a 9-millimeter in his hand. I didn't even know that my father had a gun. I was scared, confused, and proud, all at the same time. The good—my father was protecting our home, just in case the robber looked at my ID and wanted to come and try something. The bad—I had been robbed and was experiencing all of the emotions that come with feeling violated. The ugly—my father was in animal mode, motivated by his desire to preserve, protect, and guard what he held most dear—his family.

As men, we do some not-so-pretty things, and we do these things for reasons that are valid to us. We do these things to uphold a certain image or to help someone in dire need. We do these things because we feel that's what men are supposed to do. So oftentimes, ugly or bad things are done with an attempt at establishing a greater good. Now, what that greater good might be depends on the man we're talking about. But all in all, when it comes to relationships and dating specifically, you need to watch your man in how he deals in these three circumstances. How bad is his bad, how ugly is his ugly, and is his good really good? And how do you react when he's dealing with his bad, when he's looking ugly, and while he's giving you his good? Always love your man—through thick and thin. And show compassion, neither him nor you are exempt from the good, the bad, nor the ugly

LIFE COACH NOTE
by Pervis Taylor

Bishop Dale Bronner has always said inherent in every man is a king and a fool, and which one emerges depends on which one you speak to. Everyone has multiple sides. I do think it's healthy, especially in relationships, for you to be able to see the good, the bad, and the ugly in your mate. I always tell my clients with children who are a little unruly that they need to see the crazy just once to know that they can go there. Let's face it: we are flawed human beings who come from various backgrounds and experiences. Some of us are even born with certain dispositions to things. Some of my clients' depression runs in their families and others have mental illnesses in theirs. Reality is about what you can deal with, because everybody comes to the table with something. We all have some great things about us, and that's easy to accept. But where we find the challenge is in the ugly things that we have inside of us. We all have ugliness inside of us. It doesn't make you a bad person if you choose to not go further into a relationship because you can't handle another's ugly. However, know that no matter how pretty the package may look, inside is something that you will not like. We must rid ourselves of the fantasy that a perfect man exists. But what you can pray for is a man who is willing to work on the ugliness in his life. If you find that in a man, ladies, you've found gold. The best thing to do right now is to know going forward that someone is coming with baggage. The question is what can you handle?

D<small>R</small>. J<small>EAN</small> A<small>LERTE</small>, F<small>RANK</small> G<small>ATEAU</small>, J<small>ICKAEL</small> B<small>AZIN</small> <small>WITH</small> H<small>OSTS</small>
K<small>RISTINA</small> B<small>EHR</small> & JD R<small>OBERTO</small> <small>OF THE</small> B<small>ETTER</small> S<small>HOW</small> (M<small>ARCH</small> 2015)

J<small>ICKAEL</small> B<small>AZIN</small>, F<small>RANK</small> G<small>ATEAU</small>, M<small>ATT</small> L<small>AUER</small> & D<small>R</small>. J<small>EAN</small> A<small>LERTE</small> <small>TAKE</small>
<small>A</small> <small>SELFIE AFTER INTERVIEW ON</small> NBC TODAY S<small>HOW</small> (J<small>ANUARY</small> 2015)

COVER PHOTOSHOOT AT BROOKLYN SWIRL (BROOKLYN, NY)
JICKAEL BAZIN, KEMAR COHEN, KAREN TAPPIN-SAUNDERSON,
DAMANI SAUNDERSON, TAREN GUY, FRANK GATEAU,
JEAN ALERTE, GAYNA ALERTE, BARBARA DE
LALEU, INIA ESTIAM (JANUARY 2013)

PASTOR A.R. BERNARD, JAMIE HECTOR & DR. JEAN ALERTE AT
MOVING MOUNTAINS FUND RAISER IN NYC (JUNE 2014)

GAYNA ALERTE, DR. JEAN ALERTE, FADELF JACKSON AND EGYPT
SHERROD-JACKSON AT THE JACKSON'S WEDDING IN NJ (SEPTEMBER 2010)

PERVIS TAYLOR III, DR. JEAN ALERTE, FRANK GATEAU, JICKAEL BAZIN,
PAT SUMPTER-DAVIS, KEL SPENCER, RAE HOLLIDAY, DJ FA-DELF &
ZANGBA THOMSON AT BOOK LAUNCH EVENT IN NYC (FEBRUARY 2015)

AUTHORS OF SINGLE MAN, MARRIED AT ARISE 360 (MARCH 2015)

AUTHORS WITH TV PERSONALITY/HOST OF RIGHT THIS
MINUTE BETH TROUTMAN (JANUARY 2015)

AUTHORS WITH TV PERSONALITY/HOST OF NBC's THE
TODAY SHOW SAVANNAH GUTHRIE (JANUARY 2015)

AUTHORS PERVIS TAYLOR III, FRANK GATEAU, RAE HOLLIDAY,
HOST MC LYTE, KEL SPENCER & DR. JEAN ALERTE
AFTER MORNING CUP ON CENTRIC (MARCH 2015)

6

BE HIS PARTNER, NOT HIS BOSS

Frank Gateau

According to the US Department of Labor, "Women compromised 47 percent of the total US labor force, and they are projected to account for 51 percent of the increase in total labor force growth between 2008 and 2018. Sixty-six million women were employed in the United States, and 73 percent of employed women worked full-time jobs, while 27 percent worked on a part-time basis. In 2010, the unemployment rate for all women was 8.6 percent and for men it was 10.5 percent."

Nowadays, women are generating income like men, and in some cases, they are the breadwinners and are becoming the head of the household. But some of these women's economical status interferes with their love life. They forget to leave their work life at work, and they bring it home, which results in strife with their partner.

One thing to remember is your man is your companion and you are not his boss. Some women who are bosses at work will try to bring their work mentality home, but most men will not tolerate being told what to do and what not to do by their women. Men deal with stressful situations on a regular basis, and home is the place where we need to feel safe from stress. But it becomes very difficult to deal with a woman who isn't helpful in providing a stress-free environment. A man has his role to play, and a woman should support him in doing so. In no way am I suggesting that a woman is less valuable than a man, but if both parties know their roles within the relationship, then all will be well within the relationship, and they won't cross the other person's boundaries. But if you have more drama in your relationship than happiness, then something is wrong. Maybe you're too overbearing and commanding? Maybe you're not encouraging your man to reach for new heights in his career? Or maybe you're not around to share in his victories? As his partner, you should be his biggest cheerleader and supporter. A relationship is not an individual sport; it's a tag-team event. If you win, he wins.

Are you the school-principal type, always correcting your man when you think he's misbehaving? Are you the jail-warden type, always punishing your man when he does something wrong? Do you always feel the need to correct him? Do you only focus on the negatives in every situation? If you do, then eventually your man will have two words for you—I'm gone! Why? Because you don't understand the difference between being bossy and being a boss. You have to remain reasonable and always take the compassionate approach when dealing with your man.

A few of my friends are married to women who are bosses at their jobs. Sometimes, I'm there to witness the challenges and arguments they have when battling for power. But at the end the day, it's their willingness to admit when they are wrong and their willingness to compromise that makes it work. It's a give-and-take situation. Don't let degrees, job titles, social status, and income get in your way of obtaining peace in your home. Be his constructive critic. Part of being a great partner is your ability to lead and being able to receive advice as well as take it. Yes, it's okay for you to be opinionated and expressive. But if your man doesn't agree or see things from your point of view, don't jump the gun. He might be a firm believer in logically having an educated debate to drive his point home.

Women with self-control issues are problematic, and many of them are emotionally incapable of sustaining a peaceful relationship. I've noticed that the women I've dated in the past who have emotional troubles were only trying to protect themselves from getting hurt again. They were deeply insecure creatures, hard exteriors with frail insides. I didn't last too long with them because when all wasn't well, they flipped out and showed their true character—it was like Dr. Jekyll and Ms. Hyde. When someone shows you who they really are, believe them. Your man would rather you be you than someone else. So stay authentic. There's nothing wrong with self-progression and being able to take constructive criticism.

If you have ever watched the series *House of Cards*, Frank and Claire Underwood display the perfect dynamics of what a partnership in a marriage is. No matter what happens, good or bad, they both know what their common goal is, and they stick to it and uphold that no matter what. They are aware of each other's infidelity and don't mind it as long as it doesn't affect their mission. Even though they are schemers, manipulators, and ruthless and cold-blooded individuals, they function as one unit. I am not advocating their behavior and saying to use the destroy-and-conquer method to secure a great relationship, but I am observing their mind-set and vision and how they stay committed to ensuring their aspirations and goals take precedence over anything else.

You might not know what the future brings, but know that you will get what you put in. Allow your man to state his opinions. Allow him to make decisions. Don't always challenge him unnecessarily. Show your strength by playing your part. In the song "Power," Kanye West states, "You got the power to let power go." Lay down your boss title and be what he needs you to be.

Are you a woman who fears the word *submissive?* And if so, why are you afraid to submit to your man? Is it because you will feel powerless? Being submissive will only strengthen your relationship and help it grow. It will not turn you into a slave or make you weak. It will liberate you to be admired. Submissiveness is mutual, equally shared by you and your man. No one dominates all the time. Don't bore him to death with every single detail of your day. Don't bombard him with rants and pointless gossip. Don't use him as someone only there to vent to. Share pleasant thoughts and feelings with him. That's a good way to develop a genuine friendship. Mutual respect is what great relationships are built on.

RAE HOLLIDAY

Every man wants a partner, not a boss. No man wants to encounter a bossy woman when he gets home. The thought of that is troubling. We all know how it feels being around someone who is bossy. The atmosphere is not too bright, and a bossy person never makes life easy; they only make it difficult.

If you are bossy when your man first meets you, at some point in time, your bossiness is going to put a strain on your relationship.

There's something about a condescending tone that will drive even the meekest person crazy. I know a lot of women who have had relationships with bossy men. They often took on their exes' bossy characteristics and carried that with them into their new relationships. This ensured, or so they thought, that their feelings would not get hurt ever again. But this is not good. Every relationship should come with a clean slate. And truth be told, men deal with bossy females only because they have to, but none of us want to. So if you think you have bossy tendencies, I suggest you speak to a few of your close friends, see what they have to say, and make the necessary adjustments, because if you don't, your relationships could suffer because of it. Bossiness is always a substitute for something else that is or was missing. If it has gotten to the point where it's coming out in your behavior, then you might want to deal with that before even trying to be in a committed relationship with anybody.

JICKAEL BAZIN

"Keeping a feminine approach is vital—men hate bossy females."
—Ida Lupino

Personally, I'm attracted to a woman who will compliment me, not someone who will try to change and mold me into someone I am not. I do not want to be with someone controlling or manipulative. I am a prideful being by nature. I was created to compliment my lady and, therefore, neither one of us can lay claim to being the other's leader or follower.

We live in the day and age where the traditional or societal standards for women, in regards to relationships, have changed quite drastically. No longer is the woman strictly the homemaker and the man the breadwinner. Today, both men and women share these roles, and men who still believe in the traditional role of a woman as the one who cooks, cleans, and takes care of the kids are in for a rude awakening. Although women may still enjoy and be fulfilled doing these things, as women are natural nurturers, try telling them that this is what they are *supposed* to do, and you may not get a positive response.

A large percentage of the men I interviewed on this topic agreed that having a strong, independent, ambitious woman by their side inspires them to be better men, the key element being "by their side." Is it sexy to see my lady take charge of a situation? Absolutely! Do I need to be put in my place sometimes? Certainly! However, like my mentor always tells me, in any situation where you want to effectively convey your point, it's all about your delivery.

There needs to be a mutual respect between you that is evident in how you treat each other, both in social settings and behind closed doors. If you are a boss in your career, I commend you, but remember when you get home, your man is not an employee. If you are strong willed and like things done your way realize that, in a relationship, you have to learn to compromise. If you feel that you have to take charge of everything because your man is not proactive on any level and that this is a constant issue, then you need to respectfully communicate that it's time to reevaluate your long-term relationship goals.

DR. JEAN ALERTE

"I mean, on the television, I've got to continue to be Star Jones Reynolds. And I enjoy that. But in my real life, I'm a wife now. You can't really be bossy when you're married."

—Star Jones

The society-based structure of relationships between teacher and student, boss and employee, tenant and landlord are all divide-and-conquer, authoritative systems. Everyone knows their position and most of us play our roles well. Every day, we live this model as we journey through life, and so it plays an important part in our personal relationships. But we have to be aware that we are on the same team, and there shouldn't be any competition within that paradigm. Harmony should be practiced to obtain balance, and if you are bossy, try to control your energy through willpower, and remember that pride does not help; it always hurts. You should treat your man as your partner, so you two can go far as a couple.

I've heard too many men complain about the bossy women they were either dating or in committed relationships with. And the main thing that irritated most of these disgruntled men was the fact that their bossy counterparts were control freaks who constantly needed to have control of their relationships. I don't know about you, but I would also be annoyed if my partner were this way. I believe controlling situations like this come from a lack of confidence somewhere deep within the controlling party, and if you searched into their past, you might find bad experiences that they still haven't healed from yet. So, to protect themselves from being hurt ever again, they become controlling.

Ask yourself this—are you a control freak? If so, why? What experiences from your past have you not healed from yet? Know that to experience true love, you have to be vulnerable. And if you can't deal with not being in control, I can assure you that you will struggle in any committed relationship. It's essential that you put your guard down, take a deep breath, and exhale. Take control but don't be too controlling, and also allow yourself to be controlled. See partnership as an arrangement in which both parties agree to cooperate in order to advance their mutual interests. Understand that your relationship is at stake because there is no *I* in team.

Are you ready to throw it all away, or are you ready to unite with your man to help each other grow and build up the relationship? It is in the quest for greatness that you will experience joy—great joy. I know it's not going to be easy, but you can do it, and you both will be better off in the long run. Don't allow the need to control someone hold your relationship hostage; free yourself of it by first being friends with your man, day in and day out, and don't allow negative energy to block you from establishing great communication with him. Stay positive and you will find yourself in a positive relationship filled with growth, triumph, and, most certainly, true love.

KEL SPENCER

"Marriage is a partnership not a sole proprietorship."
—Ifeanyi Enoch Onuoha

While on the road to marriage, my fiancée and I created an advice bucket. We would ask as many married couples as possible for marriage tips. And we would (and still do) specify that we don't want any cliché tips like, "marriage is work," "marriage takes communication," or "don't go to bed mad at each other." No, we didn't want anything corny like that. So, they gave us the good stuff, and ever since then, we've been able to create quite a list of insightful wisdom that we've actually been able to apply even before getting married.

One piece of advice that was borderline cliché but we liked it so we kept it was:

Although we didn't invent marriage, our marriage will ultimately be us creating and inventing something that never existed before. It may have parts and angles and goals that resemble other marriages, but there will never be another marriage exactly like ours. And with that being said, it's something that we're both building and will continue to build. Furthermore, while we're building it, it will continue to reveal new things to us, about itself and about ourselves. A task like that requires a partnership and assigning a boss or trying to be a boss in that type of equation will welcome the death of the project.

Throughout my football career, I played for some great and not-too-great coaches. But one of the greatest coaches I know I actually have never played for. His name is Dino Mangiero. Back in the '80s, he played in the NFL for six years. Standing at a muscular six foot two and 265 pounds, he is well respected on the high school, collegiate, and professional level. He is a big Italian guy with a bunch of stories, a bunch of life experiences, and a great heart. He is definitely a man's man, and his intimidation factor is strong. But when you know him, you know him. I overheard one of his team speeches while he was serving as the head of football operations for the Indiana Hoosiers. He explained to the team that some guys have natural ability, meaning no one can teach LeBron James how to jump high enough for his head to hit the basketball rim. That's a gift. Then, you have guys who may not have a high degree of natural ability but they work hard, they hit the gym heavy, and they give it their all. But it's not necessarily those things that create winning teams. The glue that holds it all together is the thing that doesn't require natural talent. The cement between the bricks is the thing that doesn't require a great deal of knowledge or hard work. What keeps it all going are the things that require attention and focus. It takes no talent and no natural ability to show up for team meetings on time. It takes no physical gift from God to take notes while in those meetings. It takes no special skill or high level of knowledge to help a teammate when he's down or to show sportsmanship to each other. I believe the same holds true for any team— including you and your man.

Most people don't realize that, traditionally, CEOs and head coaches of football teams deal more with people management than project management. A head coach doesn't necessarily coach per se. He finds a great running back coach. He hires a worthy linebacker coach. He recruits a talented wide-receiver coach, and so on. And then all of these coaches operate under the offensive and defensive coordinators, who in turn operate under the head coach. The head coach designs the system, puts people in place to run the system, and in essence, they run the organization. It's the head coach's job to observe the system and manage the people in it—and in actuality, they are on the outside looking in while also being an internal piece. They are bosses of their experiences, and in the context of a relationship, those experiences should be co-managed and cultivated without any need for the term *boss*.

LIFE COACH NOTE
by Pervis Taylor

The goal of marriage is oneness. There are certain roles and responsibilities within a relationship. We as men need women. Women are very intuitive, discerning, and can see things long before they happen. There is great power in that position if you understand its value. Men do not liked to be bossed around by anyone, not even their bosses. As stated previously, the last place a man wants to feel told what to do is in his relationship. Yes, there are times when the woman may take the lead and the same goes for men. You are to become one flesh, partners, co-CEOs. With co-CEOs, there are different responsibilities, but the same goal of a profitable, successful outcome. This is not a competition or an exercise in control. It will require some time, patience, and sometimes allowing some mistakes to happen. Every man wants to feel a sense of power and leadership. We men are more sensitive than you think. To feel bossed around by our mates can incite feelings of inadequacy and emasculation. Balance is the key to life. The more you understand the delicate play of this, the more successful your relationship will be.

7

MARRIAGE SHOULDN'T BE THE END

Frank Gateau

According to the dictionary, *marriage* is "a legally sanctioned contract between a man and a woman." Entering into a marriage contract changes the legal status of both parties, giving both husband and wife new rights and obligations. Public policy is strongly in favor of marriage based on the belief that it preserves the family unit. Traditionally, marriage has been viewed as vital to the preservation of morals and civilization. Some might argue that monogamy is love, and that marriage can stand for a symbol of that, but marriage was essential used for social and legal benefits. It comes down to morals versus the legality of it. The moral part of it is "until death do us part," and sticking with that; and the legal is "we're bond by the terms and agreement of this contract and once someone fails to uphold these terms, I can opt out of this contract."

I view marriage as being a one-time thing, but I do see why some marriages fail and people separate.

Sometimes, not all things are meant to last forever. There has been a dramatic shift in the way marriages were back in the day compared to how they are now. Back in the day, arranged and fixed marriages were common; there were clear-cut definitions as to what the wife's and husband's roles were; and people married young, had plenty of children, and stayed in marriages despite being unhappy, divorce being deemed shameful and seldom an option. Nowadays, couples marry based on love and at an older age; they have smaller families; and roles are often shared for the common good of the union. But those same things have caused the foundation of marriage to become more fragile and made people think it's optional to stay in.

I can recall countless times when older men have told me to avoid marriage at all cost and remain single for as long as I can because, they said, "Once you settle down, it's over!" I found that statement to be funny and freighting at the same time. In fact, I laughed when I was being told that, but the message they were conveying was as serious as a heart attack. Now, after years of relationship experience under my belt, I understand why those men were trying to warn me about settling down. Because of them, I was a tad bit skeptical when it came to being in a commitment relationship.

"Men marry women with the hope they will never change. Women marry men with the hope they will change. Invariably they are both disappointed."

—Albert Einstein

Oftentimes, years after being married, some women will let themselves go, so to speak. They think their physical appearance doesn't matter anymore. They simply do not want to look the best that they can look. But I must say this—not looking your best most of the time is not the way to go. You must remember the first time you and your man went out on a date. How did you look? The first time you had sex with him, what did you do? Do you remember? Don't lose your attractiveness. Of course, we naturally change over time, but that doesn't mean you should stop taking pride in yourself. Today, there's a huge increase in fitness and healthy living, so you and your man should encourage each other to be fit—the couple that works out together stays together. Make your man feel desired, and he will desire you. Show him that you are still attracted to him by initiating intimacy.

"Do you know what it means to come home at night to a woman who'll give you a little love, a little affection, a little tenderness? It means you're in the wrong house, that's what it means."

—Henny Youngman

Miscommunication is the biggest problem plaguing relationships. Even though I am not married, I've realized through observing married couples that communication is not about the other person understanding you; it's more about being able to handle how the other person feels and think. The breakdown happens when you don't like what the other person is saying or not saying. We communicate both verbally and nonverbally. Learn when to speak and when not to speak. You need to fully comprehend what is being said before answering. Understanding is key to stability.

I remember when I was in middle school, there was a teacher that all the boys liked. She kept herself glammed up twenty-four seven, every single day. Her hair was always done, makeup on just right, wearing an eye-catching dress that extenuated her curves, high heels, and dazzling accessories. I can definitely say I appreciated the beauty of women at a young age. One year, there was a male teacher who began working at the school. He was a well-groomed gentleman himself. He always came to work in tailored suits, crisp French cuff shirts, vibrant colors, and polished shoes. Their styles complemented each other, and they hit it off. They began to see each other and got married two years later. Immediately after she got married, she made a complete three sixty as far as how she carried herself, and I mean exactly right after—in less than a year. Now, every day, she wore her hair in a ponytail, no makeup, a XXXL sweater, sweats, and flip-flops, not to mention she gained a couple pounds, and by "couple," I mean a lot. And it wasn't like she had just given birth, so I didn't understand where the excess weight gain came from—maybe because she was extremely happy. I wondered how someone could change so drastically in such a short period of time. I felt as if the male teacher had gotten bamboozled, and that she should have been sued for false representation. It was like she had prepared herself to catch him, but afterward, she didn't care anymore because her main goal was obtained. Imagine buying a brand-new car, and before putting a hundred miles on it, it breaks down. The warranty is expired and you're just stuck with it. That's horrible. Marriage is supposed to be a marathon not a sprint. So, never allow a marriage to be the end.

RAE HOLLIDAY

Most girls envision a dream wedding. They have grand ideas of what they want their weddings to look like, and as they grow older, they begin to add intricate details to the dream—the dress, the bridesmaids and the color of their dresses, flower arrangements, food, the reception.

Much of the time, a woman's wedding is visualized way before it actually takes place. Finally, she is married to her Prince Charming, but then there is a big question mark as to what to do after the honeymoon is over. All her life she's been planning her wedding day but hasn't given a single thought on how to maintain the new relationship with her husband.

The key to having a successful marriage is actually planning what to do after the wedding. You should treat your marriage as a business. Create a five-year plan. Write down what you and your husband expect, and also describe what you and him are going to do to meet those expectations.

You should make a note of planned trips and the funds that will be used for those trips. Will you and your man be using joint or separate bank accounts? Write everything down. Negotiate what you want. Put it in writing: *I want private time set aside for my friends.* Be blunt and straight to the point: *I want us to spend such and such time together with the children.* Create a contract now to have peace of mind later.

Don't get married just because your girlfriends are all married with children, and you don't want to be left out of the loop. Get married because it's the right thing to do. Marrying someone for the wrong reasons will ruin your destiny. Imagine coming home to a dull and boring life, somewhere you don't want to be. When the thrill is gone, trust me, your man will be gone also. I urge you to do your research on married couples. Find out what the successful ones are doing right and avoid the mistakes of the ones that got divorced. Believe it or not, marriage is only the first chapter to your book of love. There are many more chapters that need to be written, so think ahead and plan diligently.

JICKAEL BAZIN

"By all means marry; if you get a good wife [or husband], you'll become happy; if you get a bad one, you'll become a philosopher."

—Socrates

Summer has always been my favorite time of the year, and there was one particular summer that was extra special. I was set to marry the love of my life. You know the saying, "When you know, you know." I knew she was the one. At least with all my heart, I felt I knew. She was the lady I wanted to spend the rest of my life with. The one I envisioned starting a family with, and that summer, it became a reality. I was getting married because I believed in the sacrament of marriage and in the traditional path to building a family and a home.

This day was undoubtedly one of the most fulfilling days of my life up to that point. As I stood there at the altar, waiting for my bride to walk down the aisle, I remember telling my best man how elated I was and how much I was looking forward to being a husband to this amazing woman. I could see the guests rise, and I vaguely heard the organ begin to play, and there she was at the church's doors. She was breathtaking, an angel floating down the aisle, a blessing that God had planned and favored me with. We exchanged vows and received our sacrament in front of God and our families, and we celebrated our union with them.

"You can be married, but that doesn't necessarily mean that you are ready to be someone's partner in life...that's that commitment to ride or die with somebody through every step of life."
—Jada Pinkett Smith

For me, this was a total paradigm shift, and although I knew she was the one, I still questioned my readiness to be a husband. After leaving college and entering the corporate world, I went from being surrounded by my peers to daily interactions with older men and woman, most of whom had been or were presently engaged or married. In retrospect, had I known what I know now on the subject, I would have contributed more to those intriguing conversations and inquired about how they defined marriage based on their experiences, but I just listened and observed. I guess because at that point in my life I knew I wasn't ready to go to that next level, I didn't ask. One of my colleagues asked me, "Do you want to get married?" to which I responded, "I do, but not yet, maybe be in four or five years." I was twenty-two at the time. I remember the divorced one saying, "Don't do it," the married ones saying, "It's the best thing ever" and also "Don't do it," and the engaged one being excited about the preparations and saying, "I can't wait."

The one thing I did do after hearing all these different opinions from them and others was seek answers that would help me define what marriage means to me. I observed and took mental notes on couples in my family who had been married for over ten years, and every now and then, I would question them, when appropriate, on different actions and reactions I had witnessed. They spoke of things like compassion, understanding, sacrifice, loyalty, and unconditional love—things that are more than just words, and without them, you cannot have a successful marriage. Being a married man at twenty-four, I looked forward to the future with my wife.

I never looked at marriage as being the end but rather as an opportunity to enhance, share, and grow.

DR. JEAN ALERTE

When two people are married, one should not place the other in a compartment in his or her mind based on that person's own experiences or expectations. Both parties should realize that they have now merged into one and are living one vibrational energy. So, when you are weak, your man feels your weakness, and when you are strong, he is also robust. Balance is key. By working together, you can beat the odds easier; when one succeeds, so does the other.

Love is your birthright—to love and be loved. You shouldn't fear commitment because true commitment consists of loving and being loved unconditionally. You should never put love in a box. Love is universal. There are no limits to love. Love is bigger than us.

Marriage is not the end; it's the beginning, the start of a great journey. Never look at what is; instead, always look at what could be. Holding back your feelings can stop you from getting hurt, but it can also hold you back from discovering the full experience of connecting with another's heart. It is easy to steal something from someone if the other person does not know its value. No one likes to be placed in a box based on another person's perceptions. Recognize your man as an individual and respect his ideas. Love him freely, wholeheartedly. Be aware, and recognize him as your partner for life. Together, you and your man can move mountains and steamroll obstacles. Think of yourself as gaining an opportunity to fully explore the closeness of another's soul—something you connect to in many ways that you can't describe but can feel. This is the beginning of a journey, a bond, and a union of the heart. We say we fall in love, but the key is to rise in love. Find ways to be creative in your relationship, and try not to get distracted by other things that can end up being a time trap. Create a bubble of insulation for your marriage. You both have the ability to live life like it should be lived—blessed and without strife. Discover and explore your passions in life with each other and this will lead you to your true purpose.

KEL SPENCER

"I feel grateful to be part of the team. I feel grateful to be alive and living in Los Angeles. And I'm

*guaranteeing everybody here, next year we're gonna
win it again."*
~Coach Pat Riley;
1987 Lakers Championship Parade.

While growing up in New York City, one of my goals was to work for a program called Summer Youth, which was a government-funded program that helped inner city youths work summer jobs. Applicants would get to choose from over sixty locations, citywide (such as hospitals, plants, recreation centers, office buildings, etc.), and after picking a location and filling out the application, applicants as young as fourteen could start working for twenty to thirty hours a week.

For three summers straight, I worked in the psychiatric recreation unit at Kings County Hospital in Brooklyn. My duty was to hand out basketballs, games, and fun stuff to the mental patients during supervised recess hours. In a six-hour day, only two to three groups of patients came in to play for forty-five minutes at a time, so I had a lot of free time on my hands. It was basically free money. My supervisor Mr. Jones, a sixty-five-year-old light-skinned man who stood about six feet three, had photos in his office of when he had served in the army. He was a jazz guy. He played in the ABA for a year and went to college on a fencing scholarship. He was also heavily into chess and telling stories. It was the perfect symbol of a black Renaissance man, and he had achievements in both the mental and physical arena. I was intrigued. It was my father who taught me to play chess, but Mr. Jones showed me the medieval significance and meanings behind the chess pieces and how they move.

One day, we started to talk about the queen piece. We started with how to protect the queen, and that conversation led into him giving me advice on girls and relationships. There was one specific chess match between us in which my only powerful piece left was the queen. But just before we got to that point, he called that stage of the game "the honeymoon." I asked why he called it that, and he explained that most people only have a halfway view of what the honeymoon is. They look at it as a time for newlyweds to chill and relax, a time for them to be alone, to engage in marital intimacy and so on. But the other half, which people miss, is that it's also the calm before the storm. The honeymoon should be full of prayer, meditation, focus, and discussion because marriage will always be under attack. Satan doesn't want to see people happy, and as long as you are working toward happiness, you will be attacked. Mr. Jones attacked, captured my queen, and then checkmated me three moves later.

At the Lakers' 1987 championship parade, Coach Pat Riley said, "I feel grateful to be part of the team. I feel grateful to be alive and living in Los Angeles. And I'm guaranteeing everybody here, next year, we're gonna win it again."

I can only imagine what Magic Johnson felt like when he heard Pat Riley make that guarantee. I mean, you're smack-dab in the middle of celebrating—champagne, confetti, and the whole deal. It is the end of the season, the finish line, and in an instant, one simple statement turns your finish line into a starting block. However, Pat Riley making that statement was a genius move. It left little room for relaxation and complacency. We're most vulnerable to failure the day after a victory because we let our guards down. But that wasn't the case with the 1987 Lakers. If you can get your hands on the footage of the Lakers' 1988 season, you will see that they were even hungrier than they were in 1987. That's what I'd like to do. Since I was fourteen, I've looked at the honeymoon the same way, and you should too. As much as it may be a finish line and a time to enjoy a recent accomplishment, both the wedding and the honeymoon are indeed starting blocks—a brand-new beginning and a time to rest before applying all that you have learned.

Life Coach Note
by Pervis Taylor

In "The Cosby Show", the thing that was so spicy about Cliff and Claire's marriage is that they both pursued each other. They both had the same mind-set and knew that it was up to them to keep the relationship exciting. It has been said that the man needs to continue to date his wife. It's equally important that the woman continue to get excited over her husband. I emphasize keeping the romance alive in marriage because the changes of life will do their best to tear your marriage apart. Marriage is almost a joke to many people today. It's important to keep in mind the reasons why you got married. The wedding is a day, but the marriage is a lifetime. There will be many forces doing their best to separate what God has joined together. Life is a fight for territory. If you settle, what you don't want to happen is bound to happen. But if you are willing to be on the offensive and get prepared, you'll have a satisfying marriage. Marriage isn't the end; it's only the beginning of an exciting journey. It's also more fun knowing that someone is on the journey with you.

8

CHOOSE YOUR BATTLES WISELY

FRANK GATEAU

Picking your battles wisely shows that you are sensible. Nobody likes a woman who is always confrontational and, whenever she is challenged, feels the need to prove to her man, and to the world, that she has a voice, a woman who wants to be heard for every single reason and every single chance she gets. But not every battle needs to be fought and not every battle needs to be won. Unnecessary bickering and fighting is annoying. If the situation doesn't affect you personally, don't bother fighting fire with fire. Ask yourself: Is it really that important, or can it be overlooked? Develop a system that helps you know when to cross the line and engage, and when to let it go. Remember, for every action, there is a reaction. Of course there will be things that you will feel passionate about, but don't let anger cause you to be irrational and don't retaliate without thinking things through. Don't hold grudges. Don't just argue for the sake of arguing. You should want to stir up good emotions, not negative ones. With experience and time, you should be able to develop a sense of knowing when fighting a battle will be detrimental and when it will be good for your situation.

Are you fighting because you have a solution or just for the sake of hearing yourself talk? If venting or voicing your distaste doesn't improve the situation, then what are you really venting for? That sounds like you have an internal conflict. Aim to speak out with a purpose that's beneficial to your circumstances. Having a solution eases the anger and emotional stress of trying to resolve a conflict. Learn what exactly prompts you and your partner's hostile reactions, so you can better manage the altercations. That way, you can control the situation before it turns into a dispute. Never fire shots unless you are prepared to take them as well.

"Any fool can criticize, complain, condemn, and most fools do. Picking your battles is impressive and fighting them fairly is essential."

—Dale Carnegie

Take yourself out of the picture and evaluate the situation from the perspective of someone looking in. Differentiate the big things from the small. You might feel the need to prove how strong-minded you are, but there's no need to win every fight. To put it bluntly, every fight doesn't even need to be fought. Constant arguing only creates wounds that cannot be healed. If there are issues that need to be resolved, resolve them. Don't wait until the problems worsen to address them.

You and your man will have different points of view. Be understanding about what he values. When you approach him with a problem, make sure you already have the solution. You don't always have to have the last word. Remember, a woman who constantly complains is annoying. Be at peace even when things aren't going your way. Everything doesn't need to be analyzed. Let the minor stuff go. It's not worth losing your peace over. Focus on what your man is doing right, instead of things he does wrong. Learn to forgive and don't assume. Always strive to be the bigger person, and once your relationship feels like fun and not work, it means you're heading in the right direction.

"A wise woman puts a grain of sugar in everything she says to a man, and takes a grain of salt with everything he says to her."
—Helen Rowland

Sometimes you and your man will bump heads. That's inevitable. When your egos collide, what will the outcome be, victory or defeat? Is it just a matter of time before all hell breaks loose and you're wondering what happened? Instead, you and your man could be in heaven, sipping on pink lemonade and Ciroc. Life is what you make it. Your relationship consists of what you and your man are contributing to it, so make it your business to avoid arguing at all cost, and know the difference between a real problem and something minor.

Find the root of the problem and solve it. Don't allow stress to alter your personality; have patience; and take your time when dealing with issues. No relationship is perfect. We all have flaws. If your standards are too high, adjust them to fit your current situation and don't set yourself up for failure. Don't be a hypocrite. Don't criticize your man for things that you do also. Choosing your battles is a skill that requires practice, just like anything else in life, and once you start to do it effectively, you will see the rewarding results in your relationship.

RAE HOLLIDAY

During the process of getting to know your man, when you're getting to know his strengths and weaknesses, pay close attention to his weaknesses. Weaknesses are weaknesses for many different reasons, and sometimes people who are weak in certain areas are weak because of things that happened in their past. Some people are weak financially because they weren't taught money management, so they don't know how to save, so be careful when choosing your man. Make sure he has a great understanding of how finances work.

Choose your battles wisely, and never ever fight every battle. You will get exhausted and, worse, scarred for life. A wounded lover usually ends up on the injured reserve list, so don't let that happen to you. Learn to build and not destroy, even though sometimes destruction is necessary in order to build.

When you fight the wrong battles, you risk everything you have worked hard for. So, if your man has anger-management issues, gently make the suggestion for him to get help. Stay consistent in telling him that he needs to get help, but do it submissively and not intrusively. Help him get to the bottom of his problem by making him feel that his problem is your problem. This will encourage him to seek help.

JICKAEL BAZIN

Arguing and fighting are major turn-offs. Both are extremely draining and will put a strain on your relationship. Most of the time, couples don't even remember what we are arguing about. You might wake up in a bad mood and realize that today is going to be a long day. On days like this, your strength and resilience will be tested. You have no idea when this day will come, but it will come. Whether you pass or fail depends on how well you react to the situation.

> *"Choose your battles wisely. After all, life isn't measured by how many times you stood up to fight. It's not winning battles that makes you happy, but it's how many times you turned away and chose to look into a better direction. Life is too short to spend it on warring. Fight only the most, most, most important ones, let the rest go."*
>
> —C. JoyBell C.

Your man might argue with you about dirty dishes being in the kitchen sink. On these occasions, remain calm. You don't want a campfire to spread into a forest fire. All of us have pet peeves, that one thing that sets you off. For your man, it might be cleanliness, and when he sees dirty dishes in the sink, he might lose his mind. At first, your argument started out about dirty dishes, but if you two are not careful, the argument could lead into a full-fledged war. If this is so, then your reaction shouldn't be, "He said this and he said that, so I'm going to do this, and I'm going to do that to get back at him." No. By any means necessary, you must remain positive. Say you asked him to meet you somewhere and he didn't show up, and then, instead of hearing his reason why, you assumed the worse. *He didn't show up because he doesn't care,* or *Every time I count on him he's never there.* You begin to stack one negative assumption on top of another, and next thing you know, your mind is boggled. You could have avoided going in this direction if you only would have opened your mind to all possibilities. So don't assume, because when you assume, nine times out of ten, your assumption will be wrong.

DR. JEAN ALERTE

Love comes naturally. However, it's the negative thoughts that change people's thinking. Your beliefs determine your thoughts, and your thoughts determine your actions. Your perception has a huge effect on how you feel and how you react. Communication should be smooth; you should be able to disagree with your man and not raise your voice or get violent. But sometimes people can't control their emotions and their willpower is nonexistent.

It's healthy to debate, but negativity is sown when you attack. You can win a battle without throwing a single punch or speaking a single word. The battle is won in the mind, and the wise realize that and win.

You must refrain from speaking harshly, because if you don't, negative words will worsen the situation.

"Sticks and stones may break my bones, but words will never hurt me" is not factual. Mental and emotional wounds create destructive feelings. Always seek to solve the problems within you first and foremost, before going into battle with your man. Don't develop a habit of putting the blame on your man; take responsibility for your role and any wrongdoing. Don't let anger build a home within your heart. Be aware of anger when it first starts, and be careful of rage, which follows later. Rage doesn't care about anything in the given moment. Replace it with love every time it starts to take root in your heart, and learn the art of disagreeing with each other without fighting. If you get angry with your man, you should take a deep breath, count to ten until you are calm, and then think about what you want to say. Then visualize the impression your words will have to determine the best way of expressing your upset. Say what you want to say in a calm and respectful way. You can be serious, but you should also be sincere. By being self-aware, you understand the impact you have as an individual who can make things happen. You have the ability to affect others and set standards that will be followed. Follow these steps to set a tone of clear communication with your man, and you will develop a healthy, communicative relationship.

Kel Spencer

"Choose your battles wisely. After all, life isn't measured by how many times you stood up to fight. It's not winning battles that makes you happy, but it's how many times you turned away and chose to look into a better direction. Life is too short to spend it on warring. Fight only the most, most, most important ones, let the rest go."

~C. JoyBell C.

Floyd Mayweather Junior is one of the greatest fighters of our generation, and arguably the greatest of all time. But one of the critiques about him is that he has been dodging Manny Pacquiao, whom, some say, would probably be the one to give Mayweather his first-ever professional defeat. I don't know how true that is, but what I do know is Mayweather is selective in choosing his fights, as he should be. You get to a point in your career when each fight needs to be worth it, not just from a financial standpoint but the relevance of the fight in relation to your brand must also be weighed. If he wins, how big of a win is it? But if he loses, how big of a loss is it? What city will he fight in? Are the promotions intact? What do the pay-per-view splits look like? Who is going to film and air the preparation of the fight? How much time will he have to train? Will he need to gain or lose weight for the fight? If so, how much? And so on.

All of these things and more need to be factored into the equation of whether or not to take on a fight. Ultimately, you want to win. But aside from the wins and losses, there are plenty of other intricate parts to consider.

One major part is collateral damage, which means that you and your man are going to get into a verbal altercation/fight, and regardless of who the winner is, there will probably be broken furniture, etc., when you two are done. All of these broken items are considered collateral damage—stuff that got smashed during the altercation—and subconsciously, there are also damages that aren't even visible to the eye. And trust me when I say this—invisible damages are oftentimes the worst kind.

I remember a friend of mine used to date a young lady, and at one point in time, they got into a disagreement and she called me to intervene. Her main complaint was that she hated the way my friend debated and argued. She felt getting the win was more important to him than them coming to a mutual understanding. She realized during their debate that she was wrong. All of their back-and-forth dialogue allowed her to see that her perspective was off. But she had a problem with the sarcasm, the tone, and the aggression he used when they debated. She felt his behavior was uncalled for, and in her eyes, he had a bad habit of always doing things that way. It was almost like he wanted to win the argument and make her feel stupid at the same time. That damaged their path of communication, and from that point forward, she kind of held a lot of stuff in, refusing to voice her opinions because she wanted to avoid an argument. So, being the mediator, I told my friend the harsh truth about himself. I had overheard them debate and argue a few times, so I didn't need to let him know that she and I had a talk. But I did let him know that the value of his win decreased the moment when the collateral damage in his relationship increased. So, if you know that your favorite china cabinet or plasma screen will get damaged during a debate/fight between you and your man, will you participate in that debate? I would guess probably not. That would be a foolish thing to do. Remember, there's more to fighting than just the fight itself.

I can think of things within my own relationship that I would be 100 percent correct in pointing the finger at. And my fiancée would probably say the same about me. But in the larger scheme of things, I like my china cabinet and my plasma screen, so every battle doesn't need to be fought. When it comes down to it, the biggest battle actually happens within us, in being mature enough to decide which ones are really worth fighting. So choose your battles wisely.

LIFE COACH NOTE
by Pervis Taylor

Not everything is worth arguing about. Not everything needs attention. Too often in relationships, we allow little things to become the focus of our issues. It's important to remember you are in a relationship with another human who has a unique experiences and a perspective different from yours. He may not see things the way you see them; he may not understand the importance of a particular situation and vice versa. It really takes a great deal of compromise to be able to go on a journey with another person. Keeping that in mind, there are going to be times of conflict and disagreements. However, knowing when to address certain issues and when to let some things go is vital to your success. The hardest thing to do is feel like a coward in a situation, but in those instances, you have to look at the bigger picture. Marriage and relationships require both parties to be visionaries. Some things are truly just not worth the time to address. Leaving the seat up versus not paying the mortgage? Which is the weightier issue? Again, it's important to be able to discern what is going to have a greater effect on the relationship. Letting some things go doesn't make you weak. It makes you mature.

9

IF IT'S NOT BROKEN, DON'T FIX IT

FRANK GATEAU

Sometimes, a woman will feel the need to change her man, but men are creatures of habit. The good and bad habits he possesses are his and his only to fix. Only a life-altering situation can change that. Not you. So, stop wasting your time trying to change your man for the better—according to your standards. At the end of the day, it's up to him to make changes. You can help him make those changes, but that's all you can do—help.

> *"If we could change ourselves, the tendencies in the world would also change. As a man changes his own nature, so does the attitude of the world change towards him… we need not wait to see what others do."*
> —Mahatma Gandhi

The problem is you are making the same bad decisions and getting the same failed results. Nothing good happens by force, so let things flow naturally. Change doesn't happen overnight. Don't drive yourself crazy trying to fix every little problem; you will scare your man away. Stop overanalyzing everything because overthinking will create issues that are not even there. Stop comparing your relationship to your friends' relationships, because no two relationships are alike. If your friends are having problems in their relationships, don't let their problems become yours; misery loves company, and sooner or later, you might find misery in your relationship.

Remember, fixing something that doesn't need fixing is foolish. Who you are now might not be who you will be years from now, but don't allow those changes to pull you and your man apart. Make a great effort to evolve. There's no magical formula to make a relationship work; the success of your relationship depends on how much work you and your man are willing to put into it.

RAE HOLLIDAY

I have a thirty-year-old iron that's been passed down from generation to generation. It's the best iron I've ever had. When I iron my clothes, they look as crisp as clothes from the dry cleaners. My iron makes a little bit of noise and can sound a tad bit annoying at times. However, it does an amazing job. Every time my friends come over to my house, they ask, "Is there someway you can fix your iron's annoying sound?" or, my favorite, "Why don't you just get a new iron while you're at it?" But why should I listen to them and fix what's not broken? I personally think that the noise my iron makes is a small price to pay for the amazing job it does on my clothes. I believe some things are better left alone.

The example of my iron is how I feel about relationships. When you're in a committed relationship, I believe you have to formulate a system for everything. If you're going to share a bank account with your man, formulate a system about how much can go in and how much can come out. If you and your man have children, and both of you are working parents, formulate a system about how each of you will get to work and how each will pick up the children. Create a system that works, and if it's not broken, don't fix it.

Many times, people read self-help books or watch Oprah or Iyanla Vanzant to get advice. Then, something pops into their minds, and they start thinking, *We should start doing what Oprah and Iyanla said.* But what that does sometimes is cause a rift between you and your man, depending on how willing he is to try these new ideas.

Sometimes, he will want to try it because you want him to, but the only thing that does is cause a seventy-thirty dynamic. If your man does it of his own free will, then that's a fifty-fifty dynamic. It's a lot to think about, but it's worth it. When it's a seventy-thirty relationship, the person who is giving thirty is not really giving much, and the person who is giving seventy will start to get agitated because their partner is slacking. Upgrading is necessary in keeping your relationship alive, but when that time comes, you and your man should be doing the upgrading together. Problems should be solved as a unit and not separately, and you shouldn't walk away from this book thinking that it's not a good thing to upgrade, because it is. If you are willing to upgrade with your man, more power to you, because you have courageously taken another step forward—toward securing a happy relationship with your man.

JICKAEL BAZIN

As far as I'm concerned, the most consistent characteristic that we share as human beings is that we are flawed. We all possess flaws in one way or another. Therefore, why would you expect a flawless relationship? What you should keep in mind is this—don't look for the perfect man, because there aren't any perfect men out there.

Secondly, you should invest in someone who complements your values and goals, and make sure you and this person have a mutual vision of where your relationship is headed.

Just like life, relationships have their seasons. You and your man will go through good and bad times, and during the difficult moments, have patience, because cruel times are meant to test how committed you are to your relationship. Unless you are looking for a way out, don't let these tests lead you to fall victim to other men's advances or outside influences. Part of your commitment to your man is to preserve what you and he have built and, more importantly, to use your trials and tribulations as learning experiences. That's how you win in the long term.

All of the couples I've interviewed who've been in long term relationships—married for ten years or more—stated that during their rough and trying times, they were committed to each other.

I interviewed a married couple who was celebrating their thirty-third wedding anniversary. I asked them if they could go back thirty-two years and completely erase the negative moments—the times when their marriage was at its lowest points—would they do it? They answered, "Absolutely not! Our lowest moments were a blessing in disguise. During those difficult times, we learned a lot about each other, and if we erased those memories, we would be erasing a historical part of us that kept us together for thirty-three years."

I know you have encountered negative moments in your relationship, but look at these moments as blessings in disguise. Persevere through them and preserve your relationship. You have worked too hard building something from scratch to just abandon it. You have a strong will, so use it to your advantage. Your relationship will take you down many roads, some smooth and some rocky; you might even come across a muddy path every now and then. But don't lose faith. Learn the lesson that is being taught, and you will grow in wisdom.

DR. JEAN ALERTE

When you can say you have done everything in your power to make your man happy, then you can make clear decisions about the health of your relationship. Don't feel as if you are at fault if the man wants out of the relationship. You must set him free. You are doing a disservice to yourself by not moving forward and along your path. Always remember, there is someone out there who would never want to let you go. You don't need to be validated; you are perfect just the way you are and possess all the ingredients to become greater. People will change when they need to. What experiences your soul requires to grow and achieve balance is going to be different from what you think you need. If you find you are constantly trying to prove your worth to someone, you have already forgotten your value. Loving yourself raises your self-esteem. However, don't take yourself too serious—learn to laugh and enjoy the beautiful things in this world. Always do what feels most natural to you, the thoughts and actions that come from the heart. Think with your heart. Never be bitter or self-centered, because givers always sleep better. When your intentions are good, you have a clear conscience. Life is a menu, and whatever you order in your life will be delivered by your actions. Sometimes, your will find people who enjoy dating, and it's absolutely their choice. However, it is important that both parties feel the same, or you are both doing a disservice to each other. When God wants you to learn something, you have to have patience, and sometimes you need to be alone. Sometimes you develop the most by traveling alone, so make your journey count. Don't spend all your time trying to find a relationship and end up pre-occupied with the wrong person when God is ready to send the right person to you.

Never be bitter about anything, and don't take anything personally. Life is too short to carry such a heavy load, so release it. Your trials and tribulations are blessings in disguise, meant to refine you into gold. Let your star qualities light up the darkness. Always think with your heart and speak from your soul. You only live once, so make sure that the life that you are living is a life that you create with love.

KEL SPENCER

"Then the LORD God made a woman from the rib he had taken out of the man, and he brought her to the man."
—Genesis 2:22

We are not here to discuss religion. But, for argument sake, let's just say that it is written that man was here on earth first, whether that man came by way of God or evolution. Man was created first, and during that time, he had a window of opportunity to sleep alone, eat alone, laugh alone, do chores alone, and discover new things alone. When the woman came about, the first thing she was introduced to was man. So, from the very beginning, man had the knowledge of how to do things on his own, whereas the woman was more inclined to do things within the context of a relationship. I don't think it's a coincidence that Adam's and Eve's characteristics are present today in modern-day man and woman.

If you look at elderly couples, the man is a lot more likely to have his own little area, where he watches the games or the like, and if you look at couples in general, the man is a lot more likely to try to deal with things internally and within himself, while the woman is a lot more likely to share and seek insight and counseling from external sources. Because of this, women are also a lot more in tune with the upkeep of relationships. Women are the nurturers, conversation starters, and the ones better equipped to handle interactions, exchanges, and the temperature of the relationship. Women are a lot more inclined to take the initiative to work on the things within the relationship that need fixing or adjusting.

> "It is He Who created you from a single person, and made his mate of like nature, in order that he might dwell with her in love."
> —Al-'A`raf 7:189

But doing the fixing and adjusting is where the problem lies. It's one thing to address issues that you're having with your man, and it's another thing to try to change him to be the man that you want him to be and not the man that God intended for him to become. If your man has that many major issues that need changing, then maybe you don't need to be in a committed relationship with him. Allow him to find himself, to grow and develop before devoting your entire life to him.

LIFE COACH NOTE
by Pervis Taylor

One of the greatest experiences when in love and in a relationship is the feeling of being accepted and understood. Everyone on earth wants to be accepted and understood as they truly are. Some women need to get the lesson early that men are not projects; they're human beings. There will always be room for improvement and growth. But those things take time and patience. Never force someone to change or try to change the relationship. The end result will always be conflict and resistance. Moreover, changing someone makes them feel that they are not good enough as is. It is a negative experience more than anything else. People and situations change once a person has a revelation. Additionally, a crisis is another stimulant that incites change. Please note: a good woman always makes a man better. Just the very presence of a good woman who is supportive, loving, caring, and powerful would cause any man with sense to want to be better. But again, everything is in the approach. Keep in mind a man's feelings and longing for acceptance. Also, weigh your options. Is the change you seek really going to take the relationship to a new level? Who benefits? Is it to make you happy or is going to make you both happy?

10

THE REASONS
MEN CHEAT

FRANK GATEAU

Many people have different ideas about what they consider cheating. The obvious is having sex with another person, but there are a lot of gray areas as well that varies based on the type of relationship you setup. Men and women cheat for different reasons; men generally do it for physical gratification and women for emotional gratification. I believe cheating is more physical than emotional when it comes to men, and until a woman's body can produce testosterone, you will never know what your man goes through on a daily basis. It's far more dangerous and worse when a woman cheats because most women do so out of a need to connect with somebody else, when the feelings are fading or gone in their current situation. A man can go out and cheat with someone they have no desire to emotionally connect with. I saw a joke that said, "A man can cheat on his woman and sleep like a baby in the same bed next to her, but will feel bad about getting a haircut from someone other than his regular barber," which I found to be hilariously funny and true. Having a girlfriend could be great, but sometimes, he might want more, and it has nothing to do with who his girlfriend is. Maybe it's a chemical imbalance that keeps him constantly on the hunt for a new woman. But if your man is guilty of cheating, he should be held accountable for his actions. Lust could be lurking deep inside his subconscious mind, and when an opportunity presents itself, there's a possibility that he will go for it.

I've seen how addictive the game of chasing and catching women is. It's the love of the hunt, the love of a new challenge, and who doesn't love a challenge? Men will cheat because, to us, it's just sex, with no real emotional attachment, so we view it as being harmless, but to a woman, cheating always has feelings attached to it. Is it my fault if I didn't have feelings for some of the women that I had sex with? Maybe they weren't the right ones for me, or maybe I wasn't the right one for them. Whatever the case may be, I knew the difference between sex and love. I might have gotten into those relationships too fast and really wasn't prepared for commitment.

Cheating can also be a way out, a way for us to claim our independence and not be attached to women who aren't what we want in the long term. But sometimes, as men progress in life and in their careers, we are exposed to a new supply of women who weren't previously available, so we feel the need to explore these potential new mates that are now accessible.

> *"Most women think cheating is 'disgusting'…until they fall for a man that likes them back; but isn't willing to leave his lover for them."*
> —Mokokoma Mokhonoana

Sex is an important part of your relationship with your man, and the lack of sex will destroy your relationship, slowly but surely. An emotionally fulfilling relationship without adequate sex is not enough, and sometimes men would rather cheat than leave. Bad sex can cause a man to cheat. You should communicate with your partner about what he likes and what turns him on. Simply ask, "What do you like?" It sounds simple because it is.

Trying to explain to a woman that her sex is subpar or whack isn't the easiest thing to do. If there's something you are not the best at, just let your man know that you are willing to learn with a smile and an eager spirit. Your man might not have the intentions of cheating on you, but temptation is sometimes stubborn, and it can dilute your man's brains with impure thoughts. An opportunity might present itself in a platonic state, and just like that, your man could get tangled in a web of infidelity. He wasn't looking to cheat on you, but he is too weak to resist the temptation. Without willpower, your man will be unable to turn down sex from other women.

Sometimes, after being in a long-term relationship, when the physical attraction between a man and a woman isn't there anymore, the man or woman will find ways to satisfy their sexual appetite. Sometimes, after having too many drinks, a man might forget who he is and cheat. Yes! Blame it on the alcohol. Also, an emotional disconnect with his woman can drive a man into the arms of another woman. Cheating doesn't mean your man is a bad person; it simply means he has momentarily failed the test. He feels guilt deep within his soul. Maybe you're not stroking his ego at all and another woman is. Sex can be a drug to some.

I know men who want to conquer every woman that they are attracted to. These are just conquests; no feelings are involved whatsoever. Cheating is in their blood. The feeling of entitlement and of deserving to be with a different woman every now and then is overpowering. Maybe it's our biological programming that makes us think this way. The more women we sleep with, the stronger we feel. The thrill, the excitement of conquering a new woman becomes addictive. Having sex without love, without an emotional attachment, is a phase we all go through. I loved the women I was with, but I wasn't in love with them. There is a difference between love and lust. But is cheating worth the reward? Probably not, because the bite of dishonesty pollutes the pureness of the relationship; no man cheats with the intent of getting caught.

Frustration, lack of communication, boredom, disrespect, false allegations, being controlled, lack of power, too much power, dying chemistry, and unhappiness are all major factors that the woman has control of. Not to say that women are the blame, but they do play a role in men cheating. Women are not always the heartbroken victims that they appear to be. Some claim to have been cheated on, but their own hearts were not in the right place. They will love a man for what he is, rather than for who he is. Then, when they are cheated on, they cry wolf, when they are the ones in disguise. There's an interesting track called "Blame Game," by Kanye West on his fifth studio album *My Beautiful Dark Twisted Fantasy*. It is one of my favorite songs on the album, and it describes a situation where the guy is torn and forced between his emotions, treachery, lack of communication, heartbreak, and lack of love from a significant other, and it causes him to second-guess everything. If you've ever been in that situation, you can understand the anger and frustration that is inside one's head.

"Everything in the world is about sex except sex. Sex is about power."

—Oscar Wilde

The circle of people your man hangs around may be the cause of him cheating on you. I'm not justifying him cheating. I'm just saying his cheating isn't emotional; it's physical, and it doesn't diminish what he has with you. Also, the feeling of being neglected will cause your man to cheat. Maybe it's also science or his genetic makeup, his high level of testosterone, etc. You need to be worried when cheating becomes a conscious effort, meaning your relationship is failing or there is an addiction to stray that might be incurable. It takes a lot of work and cover-ups to plan to go and cheat, especially today, when it is fairly easy to get caught. If he's still willing to risk it all, it means he's either fallen for someone else or has just given up and doesn't care about the relationship anymore.

RAE HOLLIDAY

"Sex education may be a good idea in the schools, but I don't believe the kids should be given homework."

—Bill Cosby

Me personally, I am not a cheater. I do not see the point in cheating. I'd rather not cheat because I don't want to give my partner a heartache or headache. I am a firm believer in the idea that if you're going to hit me with five bricks, I want you to hit me with all five at the same time, instead of a brick a day. That's just how I am.

But I happen to know a cheater, a constant cheater actually. We are very cool and have had lots of conversations about why he cheats. As our friendship has progressed, I have started to pick up a few things about him and his childhood, which has led me to have a theory about why men cheat in general. The reason is lack of sex. I'm not saying every man is addicted to sex; however, men are external creatures. They don't always think with their brains. You see, my friend met the woman of his dreams. Physically, she was everything that he dreamt of, but she wasn't the sharpest tool in the shed. He was promiscuous before meeting her, and he stopped having sex with other women altogether. Over the course of time, his addiction to having a lot of sex kicked in, and he cheated. What he didn't understand was that his obsession for sex was still inside of him. He couldn't go from having sex with multiple women to just having sex with one woman. Eventually, he and his girlfriend got into an argument and ended up not talking to each other. They didn't break up; they just weren't speaking to each other. In those silent moments, all those repressed urges and all those women started to creep into my friend's mind. Unable to exercise his will-power, he went out there and had sex with other women. He didn't know how to control his sexual appetite, so it controlled him.

My reasoning for my friend cheating is that he had never really dealt with his sexual addiction; he just sup-pressed it. When you suppress something, you hold it down but never eradicate it. You can only hold some-thing down for so long before it erupts, and if your man is dealing with something similar, what he really wants to say is this, "I have sex issues that I have to deal with. Give me some time. Let me get me back together first and foremost before I move on any further with you."

JICKAEL BAZIN

"Love is an ice cream sundae, with all the marvelous coverings. Sex is the cherry on top."
—Jimmy Dean

This will probably be one of the most sensitive sub-jects in this book but still one that definitely needs to be touched on. Being unfaithful to your significant other can cause your relationship to end. So, why cheat? Simply put, cheating is the result of lust; when it comes to a woman, a man is a natural predator. He stalks his prey and pounces every chance he gets until she either gives in or ignores his every advance. That animal instinct in us is what feeds our lust and causes us to lose all sense of what is rational, and right or wrong.

A good friend of mine has been married fourteen years. He has always spoken very highly of his wife and children, and is also a God-fearing man who attends church services regularly. Recently, I noticed he'd been asking to hang out a bit more often, and he confided in me that he had begun having an affair and that, although he loves his wife, there is something missing. I said, "But this is the love of your life. What do you mean you feel something is missing?"

He replied, "I can't quite put my finger on it, but it seems like all we do is argue and fight. The fire that was once lit has now been extinguished." I didn't know how to explain it to him, but the answer was simple and obvious to me. Although he did, in fact, love his wife dearly, rather than looking for the root of his problems with his wife and focusing on resolving those issues, he chose the easy way, to avoid the pain of confronting their obstacles. When he is with the other woman, there is no arguing, no fighting or tension in the room. This other woman makes him feel wanted and appreciated. It may only be a sexual relationship, but the feeling he gets when he is with her is like an adrenaline rush. He knows what he is doing is wrong, and he has come to terms with that and is terrified at the thought of his wife finding out. In his case, he is simply looking for the attention that he is not getting at home, which then begs the question, if he is cheating on his wife because he is looking for attention that he is not getting at home, then logically, she's not receiving attention at home from him either. Has he even considered that she too is getting *it* from someone else?

The vast majority of men in relationships do not even want to think of their ladies possibly cheating on them. It's a pride/ego thing. A man who cheats is looking for someone to fulfill a part of him that his lady is not, plain and simple. Whether physical, emotional, or social, if there is an imbalance in the relationship, he will seek balance. After all the interviews and discussions on this topic, I conclude that there is no defining answer as to why men cheat, but I can advise you this, ladies: stimulate him intellectually, feed him plentifully, use your ingenuity to keep things spicy, and if he doesn't fall asleep after you make love to him, then, girl, you have more lovemaking to do.

DR. JEAN ALERTE

"What irritated me most in that entire situation was the fact that I wasn't feeling humiliated, or annoyed, or even fooled. Betrayal was what I felt, my heart broken not just by a guy I was in love with, but also by, as I once believed, a true friend."

—Danka V.

In a relationship, there will be temptations, but if you and your man are loyal to each other, then the temptations will be conquered. The man that you choose to invest your time in should have a values system that is stronger than sex, money, and drugs. He must be aware and also in total control of his mind, his ego, and any negative thoughts which emerge and that do not come from his heart. Let's face it: everyone wants to be appreciated; no one wants to feel neglected or taken for granted. So remember to always treat your man as a partner and show him that you value him. Show him you value his work effort, his creativity, his humility, his dependability, his loyalty, his family values, his funny side, his abilities in all the small but important things he does to show you that he cares about you. There are many things that your man brings to the table that add value to the relationship, and your man wants to hear this from the woman he loves. If your man is operating in love, which is always at a higher frequency, he would be aware of doing anything that would cause you pain because it will equally trouble him. When you hurt, he hurts, and the love he has for you will prevent him from letting your love come to an end. It takes a lot of energy to sustain a healthy relationship, so you have to keep from losing your cool when you disagree with your man, and you have to take the time to sit down and talk to each other like true soul beings. I believe a soul being will retain the memories of how it has treated or affected by another person. For instance, when a man becomes conscious of his behavior, it is only then that he will realize he was being driven by an unconscious thought, one that did not come from his heart and was not helping him move in the right direction. Patience is a virtue that can come to your aid when all seems lost. A man can certainly be loyal to his woman when he feels she is the right person and when the relationship is moving in the right direction.

Kel Spencer

"Men cheat for the same reason that dogs lick their balls…because they can."
—Samantha, *Sex and the City*

Her name was Jessica, cousin of Neesa, who lived across the street. She would come to visit during the summer. From ages eight to eleven, I would look forward to summertime in Brownsville, NY, because I knew Jessica was coming to visit at some point. But I was always too scared to speak to her. I just liked to watch her. She was Puerto Rican. One day, my dad took us to the McDonald's on Rockaway Parkway, and Jessica was there. My heart started to pound, and my palms got sweaty. I wasn't used to seeing her outside of summertime. So I came up with a plan—to fake a stomachache and ask my Dad if I could wait in the car. And that's what I did. I forfeited my chicken nuggets and sat in the car and waited—because I didn't want my dad and brothers to know that I liked Jessica. I was naive.

There are men all over this planet who are secretly in love with women, but they don't want anyone to know because they don't want to appear weak. And what they do is mask their insecurities through "penis-measuring contests," like figuring out who has the most money, the biggest muscles, or the flashiest car. And if you look at any beer or car commercial, the TV advertisements often feed our natural sexual appetites.

Unfortunately, when you have this type of external conditioning on top of a very real and natural desire to have or pursue sex, and you have had no lessons about self-control, you're a cheating train wreck waiting to happen. And don't get me wrong; men have been cheating since the beginning of time, so in no way am I blaming cheating on beer and car commercials. What I'm saying is this—enticing commercials are examples of external factors that feed our internal desires in an unhealthy way. And that external temptation has always been there. What has never really been there is an open forum for men to share, discuss, and create ways to practice self-control. And guess what? That is probably never going to happen. In my opinion, the difference between men and women in regards to having sex is this: women generally have sex as a way to bond with their mate, and men (outside the context of their relationship) have sex with no bonds in mind; they do so for how it feels, for the internal score of securing another notch under their belt. Because of this difference, our reasoning for stepping outside the borders of our relationships is different, and our occurrences are a lot more frequent. And to be honest, if a man has never really dug deep and thought about this, it's very unlikely that he will be monogamous. I have cheated on girlfriends plenty of times. I have done enough thinking and asking, seeking and knocking, and self-analysis to explain what I've just explained. And if your mechanic can't explain what's going on under the hood, that's probably not where you want to take your vehicle. We all need to start looking under the hood of our relationships and collectively do something about the cheating dilemma. We can't expect the influence of society to let up, so that will definitely make things difficult. We can't expect the stripper craze, the body modifications, the Internet porn, or the sexual undertones of media/entertainment to go away. That's not going to happen. But a shield of accountability and an understanding of what's really going on under the hood (in addition to transformational prayer if you're into God) is all we have. Men cheat because there's no real understanding of why they cheat—that's the bottom line.

LIFE COACH NOTE
by Pervis Taylor

Only God can give a definitive answer as to why men cheat. This is a question that I, as a life coach, get asked often. My answer is: I truly don't know. There are so many factors as to why a man steps out on his relationship. But what I do know is there is a disconnect taking place. Getting to the root of the issue may take time. But I will offer two things: one, all men don't cheat; and two, if you have the mind-set that all men cheat, that is what you will attract. There are men who have been extremely devoted to their wives and done all they could to please them, and the wives still cheated. There is no rhyme or reason. I will offer that we shouldn't judge another's ability to cheat. Given the right circumstances, almost anyone is susceptible to falling. What's most important is that both parties have healthy boundaries established with people outside the relationship. Also, it's important to foster healthy communication that involves brutal truth and honesty. Often, if both parties are extremely honest and committed to having a successful relationship, cheating is less likely to take place. At the end of the day, regardless of why men cheat, and beyond everything else, it is a choice, a conscious choice to intentionally partake in an outside relationship. Choices are powerful and ultimately have a lasting effect not only on ourselves but on others involved as well. It is a very serious issue. However, it is up to you to decide if you want to deal with that type of behavior. There are men out there who are devoted and loyal to their relationships.

APPENDED THOUGHTS

BY

Fadelf Jackson

As a young man I've always felt as if I've had an old soul, which caused me to view things from a different standpoint than most men and people in general; this is one of the reasons I hate when woman say "all men are alike" which I can't blame them to some extent. I was always quiet but had a lot to say when and if I was asked to speak. Through my years of traveling (because of being a dj) studying and analyzing different ethnicities and cultures and always being surrounding by older folks, I think its safe to say it had a positive effect on me. Where am I going with this…well, I've also dated a lot of different races, ethnicities etc. that allowed me to experience and encounter not just the dynamics within my past relationships but also the relationships within the families of the woman I was dating. I'm in my second and last marriage to a woman that I passionately adore and admire. I have two beautiful daughters and nothing but success ahead of us. I say all that to say; I believe what I have to offer is worthy of being digested.

The thing that we all want is to be loved; we want someone to love us unconditionally, unforgivably, selflessly. We all want a timeless love, a love that makes the world feel better despite our circumstances. The problem many people have with wanting to be loved in such an unconditional way is that, in some cases, we don't realize the taking doesn't reciprocate the giving. Some of you/us think; "oh he's a man or she's a woman, that's all they need" and or "they can do with or without it." Many may say they understand love but really may have never been loved the way that one is to truly be loved. What is or what has been your example of "real love," was it your dad never home but always sending your mother flowers, was it an abusive relationship that kept you involved only because you were afraid to be alone or was the love from random strangers that offered to spare any bit of time they had...The list goes on and on.

Relationships don't work on 50/50; they need to be 100/100 to really sustain trials and tribulations. They have to be built on a great foundation and in that all the elements of trust, communication, great sex, compromising, teaching, understanding and integration need to exist in order for the house, that love is going to build, to be strong and lasting.

Ladies here's a sure fire way to lose a good man; continue to emasculate him over and over again about issues that he is working on and maintaining in conjunction with everything else such as your needs and wants from him, aka kicking a man when he's already down. When a man truly loves you the power of your words can change his life, in turn changing your life as a couple. Men are stronger than you physically but emotionally many are weaker than their counterpart. Men have been armed with a mighty fist, woman have been armed with the swiftness of the tongue. Your tongue of a sword that you swing and sway so gracefully, cuts deep and leaves scars. Be mindful of the things you say in the heat of the moment or decide to use against him. The same power your words have to tear that man down could be used to build him up. Don't be the media within your household, rerunning the wrong thing he's done over and over again. If your place of position is from a point of empowerment because you are in a better position than him, your position is faulty and you are abusing your vows and or promises. If you are a woman of God, you have disobeyed and broken His law.... for the man in my opinion, despite his situation, is always the head of the house and deserves to be spoken to respectfully. Instead of always pointing out the wrongs in each other, constantly point out the positive and build each other, respect each other. Kicking a man when he's down will only make him stronger and better at being without you.

Ladies, be the type of female that your man has no problem being himself when his boys or family are around in your presence. When a man or his crew changes their persona when you arrive, you are uptight and or he doesn't like how you make him feel in their presence. When either of you continue to change your characters when either of you arrive, eventually resentment will build. If you don't like something he enjoys doing, don't do it or don't go, but don't deny him from enjoying life, especially if it's not offending you or your relationship... same goes for you fellas. Don't judge each other for having different taste. (e.g.: he's tending to you all day then wants to watch football on Mondays at the bar, don't start calling him names.) Respect each other's *me time*. You both had your own identity before meeting one another that attracted you to each other, right? Don't lose yourself in each other and forget how to be friends.

In a society where it seems sex is becoming a casual thing, genders are mixed & mingled, generation x is easily persuaded by the latest fad on TV and marriage seems to be becoming vintage and in some cases a ticking time bomb to failure. Relationships must have an open door policy of fast listening and understanding. We have to learn to respect each others space without disrespecting each other. A great amount of times it is not what you said but how you said it. Woman start cursing you out with their eyes and facial gestures, watch that ladies. Too many times we lose ourselves in the relationship and forget how to get back to being the sexy, vibrant, spontaneous, outgoing us that we once were because we engulf ourselves too much into our significant other and smother their *me time*. One of the oldest sayings that gets overlooked that can easily save a lot of relationships is "Keep doing what you did to get them in the beginning" and do more of that. One thing my brother says that I love is; "we work full time on our jobs and halftime on our relationships and wonder why things are falling apart."

In any relationship despite the familial status, we should approach the person before their title. Our character in life will also trickle over into how we value our home life. Strip your relationship from the title of boyfriend/girlfriend and or husband/wife and approach from a place of mutual respect, as in you are me and I am you. I've seen relationships fall apart because of jealously of one another's success. If the two of you are seeking to obtain the same goals on one accord and believe in the journey, don't force yourself into a position of a leader, be ok playing your position of assistant and do it well, learn your way into a better position of equality, seek to be of one mind. Don't be immaturely, eager to get to the top and not want to understand the journey of how to get there together as a team.

Although I have a lot more to say, I'm sure by now my fellow co-authors have probably touched on many of my thoughts. Make sure you allow each other to grow, don't pigeon toe your counterpart to mediocrity because it may not be your taste. Make sure you continue to keep the fun in your day to day, be good friends and better lovers. For those of you in time consuming careers, stop trying to balance life to fit your relationship, it will never work. They'll be times when it seems that one of you may have had to make sacrifices, that will eventually cause quiet resentment to build. The key is not to balance, it's to integrate, making your lives and schedules work for you according to what works for you, not societies rule book. Another important rule, if you have kids, is to remember to be husband and wife, boyfriend and girlfriend then mom and dad or whatever your status may be. A strong family relies on a strong bond between mom and dad. A strong relationship is also lasting through prayer; don't be afraid to pray together. Don't let minuscule arguments fester over into days that turn into weeks, don't go to bed without finishing an argument and saying goodnight. The little things in love matter don't let the, I love you and good morning fall to the waist side. Relationships require a lot of hard work; communication, patience, trust and understanding. If you are not a person that is willing to put in the work and time that it takes to sustain a healthy communion don't be surprised when things begin to crumble.

In closing, keep your dirty laundry and hardships at home between you two, spreading all the negative nuances that manifest in your relationship to your girlfriends, aunties and uncles will only cause more unnecessary issues that neither of you will need. Unveiling too much of each other to others may also cause irreversible thoughts towards you or your significant other from people who you love and value their opinion. It also works the other way as well; stop allowing so much "he said she said" to come between what you two have. Don't let the world of miserable people keep inviting you to dinner; don't rsvp to the judgmental meal. Learn to forgive each other and truly mean it. You want to know why the Carters, Smiths, Harris's, Wades, Obama's etc. work so well (don't say the money) they literally ride or die for each other, support each others ventures, keep it fun, keep it sexy, the ladies are always praising their man which in turn causes him to love praising her unconditionally. Relationships are best at 100/100, keep it 100.

"When it seems we have no more resolutions, despite all I may have done to you or you've done to me, Let's meet again. Let's meet again begins with intentionally pursuing your partner with the Fathers Love. Seeing pass their flaws and viewing them on continual basis with fresh eyes of forgiveness. Often times people may say there is no way I'm ever forgiving him/her for what they did to me. We must be mindful that harboring the unforgiving trait in your body clogs the heart with toxins. Your heart becomes contaminated then eventually distorts your view on life and stunts true maturity from being released in your life. True forgiveness can only be expressed thought the Fathers Love. In addition to the fathers love faith will be the main component in rebuilding a strong relationship. The company you keep during this process is going to play a significant role in determining your outcome." –Nehemiah The Redeemer

EPILOGUE

BY

ZANGBA THOMSON

It's true what they say: "You can lead a horse to water but you can't make it drink." This proverb applies to everyone under the sun. All through life, we are given keys to unlock doors—doors that prevent us from getting the things that our hearts desire. Unfortunately, only a few of us make it to see what's on the other side. The majority of us are still holding on tightly to the keys in our hands but never use them. Why is that? What good is it to know what to do and never do it? How will you ever know the outcome if you don't apply what you know? What do you have to lose that you haven't lost already? In your life, there are miracles waiting to happen—miracles that can transform your troubled relationship into a happy assembly of love—and convert you from being single into being in a loving relationship with the man of your dreams. Nothing is impossible to God. Where there's a will, there's a way, and the time is ripe to start sowing what you have read.

> *"For everything there is a season, a time for every activity under the heavens. A time to be born and a time to die, a time to plant and a time to uproot, a time to kill and a time to heal, a time to tear down and a time to build, a time to weep and a time to laugh, a time to mourn and a time to dance, a time to scatter stones and a time to gather them, a time to embrace and a time to refrain from embracing, a time to search and a time to give up, a time to keep and a time to throw away, a time to tear and a time to mend, a time to be silent and a time to speak, a time to love and a time to hate, a time for war and a time for peace."*
> —Ecclesiastes 3:1–8

Among all the scriptures in the Bible, none captures more beautifully the essence of *Single Man, Married Man* than Ecclesiastes 3:1–8, which paints the importance of timing. It is an essential element and, if understood correctly, it could result in you obtaining a healthy relationship with the man of your dreams. Therefore, know that everything that you are going through, and will be going through in the future, is only for a season, and weathering these storms by remaining positive and strong will help you develop a character so strong, that when you look in the mirror, you will see a courageous woman.

"Memory...is the diary that we all carry about with us."
—Oscar Wilde

Do you remember the bond that feverishly began out of pure romance at the beginning of your relationship? I'm pretty sure there were times when you gave your all, sowing seeds of faith, and there were times when you reaped the harvest of what you sowed. There were times when your man hurt you, when you hurt him, and times when you and him went separate ways to heal from all the hurting. There were times when he tore you down with verbal insults and times when he built you up with compassionate words. There were times when you wept for hours and times when you laughed with joy. There were rough times when you suffered losses. There were times when you celebrated a friend's engagement, a neighbor's childbirth, or a sibling's graduation. There were times when you danced the night away with laughter and times when you miserably cried yourself to sleep, times when you lost your mind over something your man did and times when you were able to gather your thoughts together. There were times when you happily embraced your man with a heartfelt hug and times when you didn't even want to sleep in the same bed as him—these were times when you had had enough and were ready to kick him to the curb. There were pondering times that made you reflect on all the good things that your man has done for you, from the way he makes you feel when you make love and the flowers he buys you, to the back and foot massages he gives you before bedtime. These are times when you had a smile on your face, times when the good outweighed the bad, and there were troubling times, when the bad outweighed the good. There were times when you religiously kept your vows sacred, virtuously upholding your faithful end of the bargain, and times when you were tempted to step out on your man. But thank goodness you courageously refused to cheat because cheating is deceitful. There were times when you wept over hurtful things that your man did to you—times when your heart was torn to pieces, times when you couldn't breathe without him and when you were able to breathe again because he did something great for you to restore your confidence in him. There were times when you wisely remained silent instead of arguing and times when you foolishly spoke your mind. There were times when you loved him with all your heart and times when you hated his very existence. There were times when you and he were at war and times when you were, peacefully, lying in bed, making love until the break of dawn. But no matter the time, you and your man lived life and gained experience.

So remember that time is constantly changing—it doesn't remain the same. I say that to say this: be prepared for your relationship to change constantly. You will experience moments when you and your man will be on top of the world and moments when you will be at the bottom. There will be peak seasons and low periods, so don't be surprised when unexpected things occur because unexpected things are supposed to happen in order for you to gain experience. How you deal with what's happening determines your level of maturity. If everything in your relationship is going great, and you and your man are enjoying each other's company, don't expect this blissful moment to remain forever; just like day turns into night and vice versa, so your relationship will also experience shifts of happiness into sorrow and vice versa. If nothing is going right, and there is no light at the end of the tunnel, know that this dim period is only for a season, and sunlight will soon burst forth and a way out of your predicament will be revealed. For better or worse, count every experience as a blessing, and know that you can win without fighting. When the rain is beating against your rooftop, know that you are in good hands—everything is going to be all right.

I strongly believe that you are more confident now than ever before, and you are ready to stroke your man's ego the right way and prepared to love and be loved by him. Your time is here. You know the good, the bad, and the ugly, and you also know how to identify the symptoms of why men cheat. You are prepared to do what it takes to keep your relationship afloat—even if that means being strong during times when your man is weak. You are no longer afraid of hearing the truth because the truth has set you free from worrying. You know how to choose your battles wisely, when to attack and when to be at peace, and every time you need encouragement, instead of picking up the phone and calling your girlfriends, you pick up your copy of *Single Man, Married Man* for answers on what to do when all seems lost.

I want to end this magnificent guidebook with Mel Blanc's famous catchphrase, "That's all, folks!" Thanks again for exploring the psyche of single, married, and divorced men and their views on the state of men and women in relationships. And always remember, no matter what: **P**ositive **E**nergy **A**lways **C**reates **E**levation. **PEACE**.

ABOUT THE AUTHORS

FRANK GATEAU

  @FRANKYKARATS

Frank Gateau is a managing partner and vp media director for Alerte, Carter and Associates, where he produces and directs video productions and branded media for a variety of businesses and professionals. For more than a decade, he has worked with major brands in the worlds of sports, high-end fashion, and lifestyle trends—including serving as the brand ambassador for Julian Casimir Jewelry. Visit www.JCFineDiamonds | www.acaunited.com

RAE HOLLIDAY

  @RAEHOLLIDAY

Rae Holliday is the co-creator and editor of the blog *Stuff Fly People Like*, the editor-at-large of *Blue Magazine*, and a content contributor to *Uptown Magazine* and AskMen.com. His branding firm, The Holliday Agency, has Jay-Z and Beyonce among its top-gifting clients, and he can be seen as a regular style expert and panelist on BET's *106 & Park*. Visit www.RaeHolliday.com & www.StuffFlyPeopleLike.com

JICKAEL BAZIN

  @MRBAZIN

Jickael Bazin is the cofounder of ACA Communications, an interactive distribution and personal development firm. A divorced single parent to his daughter, Anais, he serves as a business resource consultant for the Do Right Do Good Scholarship Award and as an analyst for one of North America's largest distribution companies. Visit www.acaunited.com

Dr. Jean Alerte

  @MRALERTE

Jean Alerte is an award-winning entrepreneur & author with a variety of work experience in the areas of marketing, management, and sales. Along with founding his Marketing company Alerte, Carter and Associates, he has produced comedy concerts and tours for acts such as Kevin Hart and Charlie Murphy. He also serves as the executive director of the Unity in the Community Foundation in Brooklyn, New York where he has given out $23,000 to high school students to attend college. Originally from Port au Prince, Haiti, Alerte currently resides in Brooklyn with his wife, with whom he opened the Brooklyn Swirl frozen yogurt shop in 2012. Jean received his Honorary Doctorate in Philosophy Humane Letters from Global ODS & University in 2014. Visit www.JeanAlerte.com

Zangba Thomson

@ZANGBATHOMSON

Zangba Thomson is the author of *Three Black Boys: Tomorrow After Supper* and *The Hotep Brother Manuscript*, as well as the coauthor of *Do Right Do Good*. A seasoned screenwriter, he serves as creative director at Bong Mines Entertainment, LLC, and as New York's life coach examiner at Examiner.com, where he contributes a wide range of motivational articles. Visit www.ZangbaThomson.com

Kel Spencer

  @KELSPENCER

Kel Spencer is an American Music Award-winning song-writer who has written for and with artists including Wyclef Jean, Mary J. Blige, and Will Smith. Recently accepted into the elite group of BET Music Matters artists, Spencer has penned culture writings for companies including *AEON Magazine*, BET, and Centric TV online, as well as a wide range of successful theme songs and commercial jingles. Visit www.KelSpencer.com

PERVIS TAYLOR

  @PERVISTAYLOR

Pervis Taylor III is an in-demand life coach, inspirational speaker, and author of the bestselling Pervis Principles book series. Originally signed as an actor-model to Wilhelmina Models, he has a background in the music and entertainment industries, but found his calling in caring for the souls of others. A contributor to the websites BlackEnterprise.com and Beliefnet.com, he is also the creator of the inspirational life coach app I-Inspire. Visit www.PervisTaylor.com

FADELF JACKSON

  @DJFADELF

Dj Fadelf, is a world traveled tour/lifestyle dj and official dj for 3x Grammy winners The Product G&B, model, songwriter and fitness trainer. Entrepreneur at heart, Fadelf is also the Owner-Operator of Luxe Sound Entertainment, a professional entertainment company that provides Djs, bands and photographers for all occasions ranging from celebrity & political events, down to private birthdays and sweet 16s. Fadelf has garnered guest, mix-show slots on New York's radio stations Hot 97 and 107.5 WBLS and featured in several notable magazines and websites. As a Philanthropist, Fleet dj and Fit Radio dj it's safe to say Dj Fadelf is a renaissance man to be watched. Visit www. DJFadelf.com

ACKNOWLEDGEMENTS

FRANK GATEAU

I would like to thank God first and foremost for allowing me to pursue my vision and my passion's. Thank you to all of the people who contributed to making this book possible. To the entire SMMM team and co-authors Jean, Jickael, Rae, Kel, Pervis and Zangba, it was a long process but we brought home the gold. To my mother and father for raising me and providing me my first glimpse of what building a foundation with someone should be like. To my sister for all her support and being the good child, and always raising the bar high for me to follow. My brother-in-law for the hours of counseling and story telling that I can't even repeat. To Jazzy and my brother's from another who's always down for a good cause Rob M, K.Smith, Keith T, Derrick O, Nick P, Byran L, Drew R, and Alix J, I salute you all. To all my family, and friends who are also family who's helped me along the way. I may not verbally express it all the time, but I love you all.

JICKAEL BAZIN

Thank you to my Lord and Savior Jesus Christ, your grace and favor made this publication possible. To the greatest blessing of my life, my daughter Anais, my happiness is dictated by your happiness, I've known no greater love than being your dad. You, Micka and Talia, truly make life an absolute joy to live. To my mother, Marlene, thank you for your support, sacrifice and unconditional love. Rackel, my sister, my best friend, there aren't enough words to describe how grateful I am to have you in my life. Thank you for your counseling, generosity and support. Love you Rackstar! Christina (ChristouBa), thank you for the inspiration. Our bond and friendship are priceless. To Jean Alerte, family first, business partners and now co-authors of SMMM. You inspire me everyday brother. Salute and thank you! Co-authors Frank (Karats), Rae, Kel, Pervis and Zangba, I love it when a plan comes together, thank you guys for a fun, rollercoaster ride, project. We made it count! To Georges and Chantal, just by watching you over the last twenty plus years have taught me so much about love and relationships. Thank you for being such great mentors and role models. Love you guys! Meko (Blackface), my man hundred fifty grand, thank you for the advice and the laughter when I needed it most! Oy Oy...Love you bwoy! My family and friends abroad and in the U.S., thank you for your influences in my life, small or large, I would not be the man I am today without them. And last but certainly not least, to you, the reader, thank you for your support and attention. I sincerely hope this book had meaning to you.

Dr. Jean Alerte

Thank you to God for never making a mistake and for placing this vision in our minds. My wife for being my source of inspiration daily. Thank you for being patient with me through those late nights. Without you none of this would be possible! My parents for showing me what a 40-year partnership looks like. Gayna and I are thankful. My father in law for the hours spent getting interviewed for this book! Your wealth of knowledge was appreciated. My Co-Creators Jickael, Frank & Rae we did it! 3 years & a lot of early mornings along with late nights going through surveys, interviews & so many testimonies. My co-authors Zangba, Kel & Pervis thank you for your contribution to this project! Lance Covington and the all the men that shared their views and stories. You guys made it complete so thank you! Barbara C. De Laleu for always believing in our vision and for pushing us! Congrats on everything & you made our book trailer come to life! To everyone on the cover David, Kemar Cohen, my wife, Inia Estima, Karen Tappin-Saunderson, Damani Saunderson.

We appreciate you all for helping us visually create our vision & thank you to Jon Ortiz for capturing our vision! Bang for an amazing cover always great working with you. Emanuel of ACA Media for a great trailer & commercial. Our graphic design & website team David, Raymond Deane & Phill Hammond. My Chief of Staff Toni Diggs for being such a blessing to me and the team, my sister Stephanie Alerte for all your support, My aunts & uncles for all your support, Debbie Louis for putting together our 1st panel at Brooklyn Swirl & brunch at La Caye. Our Publicist Jennifer Cadet for all that you do! Jamie Hector on blessing this project with the foreword, continue to bless the world with your talents and the children with your foundation Moving Mountains. All the media outlets that took interest in our project and sharing with the world DNAINFO, NBC TODAY Show, FOX, Daily Mail, 103.9 Tom Joyner & Jacque Reid, D.L. Hugley, HOT105 Jill Tracey a huge thank you!

Rae Holliday

First and foremost, I MUST thank God, for once again turning a dream into a reality, and sending his soldiers; Jean, Frank & Jickael to recruit me. My Grandmother raised me to be who she didn't have the resources to be, and my Mom encouraged me to be who she always wanted to be, it worked, and for their love and support, I dedicate my contribution to this book to them. And lastly, I would not be the person I am without the true love and support from my bevy of best friends, Panama J. Smith, Renee N. Forde, Donnell Dixon, Harlem Harris & Bernard Smalls. Thank You. Thank You. Thank You.

Zangba Thomson

Hotep to The Most High The Highest for giving me the right knowledge, the right wisdom and the right over standing to contribute wholeheartedly to Single Man Married Man; and thanks again to Jean, Frank and Jickael for bringing me on board this classic journey.

Peace & Love

Kel Spencer

I first want to thank God as Elohim, the Creator. For in your creation, you ignited the principal that it was not good for man to be alone so you created woman. And it was from that dynamic that our world is fueled to this very day. I want to thank my parents for showing me an awesome model of a marriage during my childhood years. I want to thank all of the 'sister' figures I had growing up. It was watching what guys do to make you smile and cry, what guys did to influence your conversations, your shopping, and even the way you acted, that showed me at an early age, what buttons to push and not to push when it comes to women. I want to thank the brotherhood and #SMMM team for allowing me to be a part of this project and finally, I want to thank my woman. Quana, You have been the ultimate friend, lover, sister in Christ and partner. And I look forward living out my vows with you.

Pervis Taylor, III

I would like to think my Heavenly Father for his love and grace. I want to thank my father, Pervis Taylor Jr. and my Grandmother June Taylor who are my cheerleaders in heaven. To Jean Alerte for the great opportunity. To all my devoted friends, family and supporters thank you. My mother Jacquelyn Taylor, sister Jocelyn Taylor, and brother Jerrod Taylor. I love you! My sis in law Tajare Taylor you are the best. My niece and nephews...uncle loves you. To the other brothers who helped make this vision a reality, many blessings. God is good, Pervis

DJ FADELF

I give all glory to God and appreciate the man that he continues to mold me into. I salute all the gentleman involved with this book and appreciate the fact that we could all come together and create such good content without any egos and animosity. I love that we came together to promote a good purpose, intrigue the minds of our readers and inspire others to be better. I want to send many, future thanks and gratitude to all of you that have or will buy and support this book. Big shout out to my Family for always supporting anything I've been involved with, it means a lot. I claim victory in this book and believe this is not the last one you shall see from this collection of gentleman. God bless you all.

20171960R00150

Made in the USA
Middletown, DE
18 May 2015